In nothing be anxious; but in everything by prayer and supplication with thanksgiving let your requests be made known to God.—Philippians 4:6

THE POWERFUL WEAPON OF PRAYER
A Healthy Prayer Life

Edward D. Andrews

THE POWERFUL WEAPON OF PRAYER

A Healthy Prayer Life

Edward D. Andrews

Christian Publishing House
Cambridge, Ohio

Copyright © 2017 Edward D. Andrews

All rights reserved. Except for brief quotations in articles, other publications, book reviews, and blogs, no part of this book may be reproduced in any manner without prior written permission from the publishers. For information, write, support@christianpublishers.org

Unless otherwise stated, Scripture quotations are from Updated American Standard Version (UASV) Copyright © 2022 by Christian Publishing House

THE POWERFUL WEAPON OF PRAYER: A Healthy Prayer Life by Edward D. Andrews

ISBN-10: 1945757418

ISBN-13: 978-1945757419

Table of Contents

Book Description 7

Preface 9

Introduction..11

SECTION 1 THE IMPORTANCE OF PRAYER 13

   CHAPTER 1 Being Serious and Sensible in Our Prayers.......16

   CHAPTER 2 "Lord, Teach Us to Pray" 19

   CHAPTER 3 God Gives Holy Spirit to Those Asking Him..22

   CHAPTER 4 The Father Provides Our Daily Needs..............27

SECTION 2 IMPROVING OUR PRAYERS................... 30

   CHAPTER 5 When Should We Pray?..33

   CHAPTER 6 How Does God Communicate with Us Today? 37

   CHAPTER 7 How Can We Improve Our Prayers? 41

   CHAPTER 8 Why Does God Reject Some Prayers 45

SECTION 3 PRAYERS THAT THE FATHER LISTENS TO AND ANSWERS IF THEY ARE ACCORDING TO HIS WILL AND PURPOSES... 50

   CHAPTER 9 The Father Listens to the Prayer of the Humble and the Contrite 55

   CHAPTER 10 The Eyes of the Father Are Toward the Righteous and Their Cry..63

   CHAPTER 11 The Power of Prayer—Not All Requests Are Granted..68

SECTION 4 BIBLICAL ANSWERS TO THE DIFFICULT SUBJECTS 73

   CHAPTER 12 How Can We Deal with Doubt and Unbelief? 77

   CHAPTER 13 Our Struggle Against Dark Spiritual Forces...81

APPENDIX A How Can We Reconcile Our Faith with the Realities of the World Around Us?.. 85

APPENDIX B Why Is Life So Unfair?....................................... 89

APPENDIX C How Can We Live a Life That Is Pleasing to God?.. 93

APPENDIX D How Can We Find Out What God Requires of Us? 97

APPENDIX E In What Ways Must God's Servants Be Clean? 100

APPENDIX F What Are the Practices That God Hates? ... 103

APPENDIX G What Are the Markers of a True Christian?106

APPENDIX H How Can We Help Others to Do God's Will? 110

BIBLIOGRAPH 113

Book Description

In a world fraught with difficulties and spiritual battles, "THE POWERFUL WEAPON OF PRAYER: A Healthy Prayer Life" serves as an essential guide for every Christian seeking a fulfilling and effective prayer life. This in-depth exploration does more than just scratch the surface—it provides comprehensive insights into the doctrine, theology, and practice of prayer as outlined in Scripture.

Section 1 starts by establishing the sheer **Importance of Prayer**, touching upon the sobriety and mindfulness we must maintain in our communication with God. From learning the Lord's Prayer to understanding how Jehovah provides for our daily needs, this section lays the foundation for a lifetime of meaningful dialogue with the Father.

Moving on, **Section 2** aims at **Improving Our Prayers**. When should we pray, and how can we enhance the quality of our prayers? This segment goes further to tackle a sensitive issue—why some prayers may not receive the answer we hope for, emphasizing the role of God's Will in answering prayers.

Section 3 is dedicated to identifying **Prayers that the Father Listens To and Answers According to His Will and Purposes**. Here, you'll find enriching discussions about the significance of humility and contrition, and why living a righteous life is vital for an efficacious prayer life. This section also confronts the challenging topic of why not all prayer requests are granted.

The final part of the book, **Section 4**, provides **Biblical Answers to Difficult Subjects** that are often stumbling blocks for many, such as dealing with doubt and confronting spiritual warfare.

The book is capped off with several appendices that delve into complex issues—how to reconcile faith with the world's harsh realities, understanding God's requirements, and identifying markers of true Christianity, among others.

Whether you're a spiritual novice or a seasoned believer, "THE POWERFUL WEAPON OF PRAYER: A Healthy Prayer Life" offers a comprehensive look into the subject, affirming that prayer isn't just a ritual but a powerful weapon granted to us by God for a victorious Christian life.

Preface

Welcome, dear reader, to a journey that promises to be both enlightening and spiritually enriching. As you delve into the pages of "THE POWERFUL WEAPON OF PRAYER: A Healthy Prayer Life," you will embark on a path that has been tread by the saints, apostles, and countless believers throughout history—a path that leads to the very heart of God. Prayer, in its quintessence, is more than mere utterances or ritualistic practices. It's a divine conversation, a dialogue that shapes our soul, molds our character, and etches upon us the very image of God.

The Christian journey is not one that can be walked alone. While Scripture serves as our map and the Holy Spirit-inspired Word of God as our guide, prayer is the compass that constantly aligns us to the Will of God. In this book, you won't find quick fixes, five-step solutions, or superficial approaches to prayer. Instead, you will encounter an exhaustive study deeply rooted in the Bible, aimed to facilitate a well-rounded and healthy prayer life.

This is not a book solely for the beginner, although those new to the Christian faith will find a reliable guide to forming their prayer life here. Neither is it just for the seasoned believer, although even a veteran in the faith will discover fresh insights into the depths of prayer. This book is for anyone who longs for a dynamic relationship with Jehovah, a relationship that is nurtured and cultivated through the powerful medium of prayer.

To produce a work that stands on the bedrock of Scriptural truths, I have divided this book into four key sections, each designed to address various aspects and questions concerning prayer. I have also included several appendices for an even more comprehensive understanding of related topics. My aim is that this book will serve as a manual, a spiritual toolkit if you will, that equips you to face the challenges of the modern world without compromising on the ancient, unchanging truths of Scripture.

Edward D. Andrews

I hope this book serves not just as a guide, but also as a companion in your spiritual journey. As you read through, may you find your own voice in prayer, may you understand the heart of God a little more, and most importantly, may your life become a living testament to the transformative power of prayer.

To God be the glory, now and forever. Amen.

Edward D. Andrews

Author of 220 books and the Chief Translator of the Updated American Standard Version

Introduction

The fervor and intensity of a believer's life can often be gauged by the quality of their prayer life. From the solitary confines of your room to the bustling atmosphere of a church congregation, prayer remains the unifying element that connects us to the divine. But prayer is not just a liturgical formula; it's a journey. And like any meaningful journey, it comes with its set of challenges, detours, and moments of deep introspection.

This book, "THE POWERFUL WEAPON OF PRAYER: A Healthy Prayer Life," serves as a manual for this sacred journey. But let's be clear: This is not a book you read once and then consign to your bookshelf. It is my earnest desire that the pages you are about to read will become a companion to your spiritual journey, dog-eared and worn, always within arm's reach as you navigate the various stages and scenarios of life.

The Word of God is the foundation upon which we build our understanding of prayer. The Biblical figures we will encounter in this book had their lives dramatically transformed through the act of prayer. Think about the instance where Daniel prayed with such dedication that he even risked defying the law of the land. Or consider the apostle Paul, who in the depths of a Roman prison, prayed not for his release, but for the growth and perseverance of the Church. These stories, and many more, testify to the transformative potential of a vibrant prayer life.

Yet, prayer isn't just about us. The ultimate aim of prayer is the glory of Jehovah, our God. It is a means by which we align our imperfect wills to His perfect and pleasing will. Prayer is as much about listening as it is about speaking, as much about receiving wisdom as it is about requesting help. It's the instrument God uses to mold us into the servants He desires us to be, enabling us to perform acts of love, humility, and service that transcend human ability.

Edward D. Andrews

I invite you to approach this book with a spirit of openness and a heart desirous of divine transformation. Whether you are a new believer just stepping into this spiritual discipline or a mature Christian seeking to enrich an already deep prayer life, this book aims to be your guide, challenging you to explore the untapped depths that prayer has to offer.

May you be encouraged, inspired, and led closer to Jehovah as you turn these pages. It's time to embark on this momentous journey, a journey that promises not just to change your life but to change you.

SECTION 1 THE IMPORTANCE OF PRAYER

Explore the profound significance of prayer in the Christian journey. Delve into its role in nurturing a relationship with God, interceding for others, aligning with God's will, and fortifying against spiritual challenges. Understand why prayer remains the heartbeat of a thriving Christian life.

Prayer stands as one of the central pillars of the Christian faith. Throughout the annals of Scripture and church history, we continually witness the profound impact of heartfelt prayers. But what exactly makes prayer so indispensable? Delving deeper into Scripture and the teachings of early church leaders, we find that prayer not only molds the spiritual health of the believer but also affects the very trajectory of God's purposes on earth.

The Vital Link to the Divine

Prayer, at its core, is the vital communication link between the Creator and His creation. When Adam and Eve walked in the Garden of Eden, they enjoyed unhindered communion with God. This initial setting represents the ideal relationship God desires with every one of us – one of *intimate connection* and *constant dialogue*. Although sin introduced a barrier, the ability and need for prayer remained.

A Testimony to Our Reliance on God

When we pray, we essentially admit our utter dependence on a power greater than ourselves. No matter the strength, wisdom, or resources we possess, we inevitably encounter situations beyond our control. In these moments, our prayers become testimonies, acknowledging our limited nature and the unlimited sovereignty of God. They remind us of the Apostle Paul's exhortation: "Do not be anxious about anything, but in everything by prayer and supplication with thanksgiving let your requests be made known to God" (Philippians 4:6, UASV).

Nurturing the Personal Relationship with God

Every healthy relationship demands communication. Similarly, our relationship with God flourishes when we consistently engage with Him in prayer. Just as we cherish moments of deep conversation with a loved one, our spiritual health thrives when we have these *authentic conversations* with God. Through prayer, we not only present our requests but also get to know God's heart, nature, and desires for our lives.

The Power of Intercession

The role of prayer isn't restricted to our personal needs. As believers, we're called to intercede on behalf of others, pleading for their situations as if they were our own. This form of prayer not only aligns our hearts with God's compassion but also plays a pivotal role in the broader spiritual realm. Throughout Scripture, we witness how intercessory prayers averted judgment, brought healing, and ushered in blessings. Such was the power of Moses' prayer that God relented from His anger against the Israelites (Exodus 32:9-14).

Aligning with God's Will

One of the less emphasized but profoundly significant aspects of prayer is its ability to align our hearts with God's will. As we immerse ourselves in prayer, the Holy Spirit illuminates God's Word and will to us. This transformative process shapes our desires, ambitions, and aspirations in sync with God's purposes. Jesus Himself, in the Garden of Gethsemane, prayed, "not as I will, but as you will" (Matthew 26:39,

UASV), signifying the ultimate act of surrendering one's desires to God's grand design.

Fortifying Against Spiritual Warfare

The Scriptures unequivocally recognize the reality of spiritual warfare. As the Apostle Paul advises, we wrestle not against flesh and blood but against spiritual forces of wickedness (Ephesians 6:12). Prayer, in this context, is our shield and weapon. When faced with temptations, challenges, or spiritual attacks, prayer serves as our sanctuary, providing protection, guidance, and the strength to persevere.

Expressing Gratitude and Worship

Beyond requests and intercession, prayer is our avenue for expressing gratitude, adoration, and worship. Through it, we recognize God's goodness, mercy, and grace in our lives. Every answered prayer, every blessing, even the very breath we take, warrants heartfelt gratitude. Such prayers echo the sentiment of the Psalmist: "Enter his gates with thanksgiving, and his courts with praise! Give thanks to him; bless his name!" (Psalm 100:4, UASV).

Conclusion

The significance of prayer cannot be overstated. It's our lifeline, our spiritual sustenance, our compass in the storms of life. The power of prayer doesn't lie in eloquent words but in sincere hearts that earnestly seek God. In an ever-changing world, the practice of prayer remains a constant, urging us to draw closer to our unchanging God. It's a privilege, a duty, and, indeed, the heartbeat of a thriving Christian life.

Edward D. Andrews

CHAPTER 1 Being Serious and Sensible in Our Prayers

The Significance of Sincere Prayers

Prayer, at its core, is a communication with the Almighty God. Every conversation with God should be taken with the gravity and sincerity it deserves. When we speak to God, we're not simply voicing out our desires, frustrations, or thanksgivings; we are, in fact, engaging in a divine dialogue. This should inspire a sense of awe, reverence, and solemnity.

There are instances throughout the Scriptures where individuals approached God casually or even insincerely, and they missed the genuine benefits of prayer. While God is loving and patient, He also values honesty and earnestness. The parable of the Pharisee and the tax collector in Luke 18:9-14 gives a clear contrast between a self-righteous, insincere prayer and a humble, genuine plea for mercy. It is the tax collector's sincere and contrite heart that justifies him before God.

Being Sensible: Aligning Prayers with God's Word

Being sensible in our prayers means aligning our petitions with God's will and the teachings of Scripture. It does not mean we cannot bring our personal requests and emotions before God; instead, it is a call to ensure our desires harmonize with His divine purposes.

For instance, while we might be driven by human desires to pray for material prosperity, James 4:3 reminds us, "You ask and do not receive, because you ask wrongly, to spend it on your passions." A sensible prayer life takes into account what God has revealed about His character, His purposes, and His will for our lives.

Embracing Humility in Our Approach

When we approach God in prayer, it should be with a posture of humility. Recognizing our position before God, understanding that He is the Creator and we are His creation, helps shape our prayers to be both serious and sensible. As the Psalmist declares in Psalm 8:4, "What is man that You are mindful of him, and the son of man that You care for him?" This perspective ensures that we don't approach God with a sense of entitlement but with a heart of gratitude.

Avoiding Repetitive and Vain Phrasings

Jesus himself warned against using "vain repetitions" when praying in Matthew 6:7. While there's value in persistent prayer, as shown by the parable of the persistent widow in Luke 18:1-8, our words should not become empty through thoughtless repetition. Rather, they should emanate from a genuine heart, filled with specific, thought-out concerns and praises. Being sensible in prayer also means avoiding long-winded prayers that aim to impress rather than express.

Practical Steps to Enhance the Seriousness and Sensibility of Our Prayers

1. **Daily Scripture Reading**: Engaging regularly with God's Word will naturally align our hearts and minds with His will. It offers us insights into His nature, His promises, and His desires for our lives.

2. **Prayer Journaling**: Writing out our prayers can be an effective way to stay focused, avoid repetition, and express our thoughts and feelings sincerely. It also provides a record of our journey with God, allowing us to reflect on answered prayers and see our spiritual growth.

3. **Regular Self-Examination**: Just as David asked in Psalm 139:23-24, "Search me, O God, and know my heart; test me and know my anxious thoughts. See if there is any offensive way in me," we too should regularly invite God to search our hearts, ensuring our motives in prayer are pure.

4. **Community Prayer**: Engaging in group prayers can provide a balanced perspective, as we listen to others pray and are reminded of the broader body of Christ. It encourages a collective spirit of worship and intercession.

5. **Educate Ourselves**: Books, sermons, and Bible study materials on prayer can provide valuable insights, helping us refine our approach to God.

In Conclusion

The essence of prayer lies not in the eloquence of our words but in the sincerity of our hearts. By ensuring that our prayers are both serious and sensible, we draw closer to God's heart, understanding His desires for us and ensuring that our petitions align with His divine will. Such a prayer life not only brings glory to God but also brings spiritual depth and fulfillment to our lives.

CHAPTER 2 "Lord, Teach Us to Pray"

Introduction to the Disciples' Request

The disciples' plea, "Lord, teach us to pray," as recorded in Luke 11:1, unveils a profound realization. They had observed Jesus' own intimate relationship with God through prayer, and they yearned for that same deep connection. Rather than desiring to perform miracles or preach with authority, they wanted to grasp the essence of authentic communication with God.

The Significance of Their Request

1. **Observing Jesus' Prayer Life**: Throughout the Gospels, we see Jesus often retreating to quiet places to pray. This consistent commitment to communication with His Father must have made a lasting impression on the disciples. Their request reveals an awareness that prayer was a cornerstone of Jesus' ministry and personal relationship with God.

2. **A Desire for Intimacy with God**: By asking Jesus to teach them to pray, the disciples were expressing a deeper longing – a desire for genuine intimacy with God. They didn't just want to recite words; they wanted their prayers to resonate with the heart of the Father, much like Jesus' prayers did.

The Model Prayer: The Lord's Prayer

In response to their request, Jesus offered what is often referred to as the Lord's Prayer in Luke 11:2-4. This was not merely a prayer to be recited but a model highlighting key elements for effective communication with God.

1. **Acknowledgment of God's Sovereignty**: "Father, hallowed be your name." Before any request or petition, Jesus emphasizes the sanctity and reverence due to God's name. It underscores that every prayer should begin with worship and adoration.
2. **Seeking God's Will**: "Your kingdom come." Jesus prioritizes God's kingdom and will above personal desires. Our prayers should similarly reflect a submission to God's grand redemptive plan.
3. **Petition for Daily Needs**: "Give us each day our daily bread." While the earlier parts are God-centered, Jesus also acknowledges the importance of bringing our daily needs before the Father, emphasizing dependence on Him for provision.
4. **Confession and Forgiveness**: "Forgive us our sins, for we also forgive everyone who sins against us." The act of confession and the plea for forgiveness are vital. Additionally, Jesus ties God's forgiveness of our sins to our willingness to forgive others, stressing the importance of a merciful heart.
5. **Guidance and Protection**: "And lead us not into temptation." This part of the prayer is a plea for guidance, strength, and protection from moral failings and the snares of the evil one.

Beyond the Model: Deepening the Dialogue

While the Lord's Prayer serves as a foundational model, Jesus' teachings and actions throughout the Gospels offer further insights into cultivating a rich prayer life.

1. **Praying with Persistence**: The parables of the persistent widow (Luke 18:1-8) and the friend at midnight (Luke 11:5-8)

illustrate the importance of praying with tenacity and unwavering faith.
2. **Praying with Humility**: The parable of the Pharisee and the tax collector (Luke 18:9-14) starkly contrasts the prayers of a self-righteous man and a humble sinner, emphasizing God's desire for heartfelt humility over self-promotion.
3. **Praying with Honesty**: Jesus, in His agony in the Garden of Gethsemane, demonstrated raw honesty in His prayers, laying bare His emotions before the Father (Matthew 26:39). Our prayers should also be spaces of vulnerability and truth.

Consistent Prayer: A Lifelong Journey

Like any relationship, our communication with God matures and deepens over time. The disciples' plea, "Lord, teach us to pray," is not a one-time request but a lifelong journey of learning and growing.

1. **Embrace Continual Learning**: No matter our spiritual maturity, there's always more to understand about prayer. Whether we've been praying for decades or are new to the faith, we must remain teachable, seeking guidance from Scripture and godly mentors.
2. **Engage in Regular Self-Examination**: Periodic introspection can reveal areas where our prayers might have become routine or insincere. By consistently examining our motives and attitudes, we can realign our prayers with God's heart.

Conclusion

The disciples' plea represents every believer's heart cry across the ages. The journey to mastering prayer is an ongoing process, one that requires patience, humility, and perseverance. As we seek to improve the quality of our prayers, we draw closer to God's heart, experiencing the depths of His love and the power of His mighty hand at work in our lives.

CHAPTER 3 God Gives Holy Spirit to Those Asking Him

The Promises of Jesus

One of the most fundamental promises that Jesus Christ made to his disciples is found in the Gospel of Luke. He said, *"If you then, being evil, know how to give good gifts to your children, how much more will the heavenly Father give the Holy Spirit to those asking Him?"* (Luke 11:13, UASV). This statement is profound. Despite humanity's imperfections and weaknesses, even the most flawed among us know how to give good things to our children. Jesus used this simple observation to point out a powerful truth: If imperfect humans can bestow good gifts upon their offspring, then surely our perfect Heavenly Father will give the Holy Spirit to those sincerely seeking it.

Understanding the Role of the Holy Spirit

To grasp the full significance of Jesus' promise, it is essential to understand the role and function of the Holy Spirit. While the Bible does not teach the indwelling of the Holy Spirit, it does present the Holy Spirit as a vital force from God that has various roles. It was by means of this spirit that God moved upon the surface of the waters during the creation of the world (Genesis 1:2). Throughout Scripture, the Holy Spirit is shown guiding, empowering, and influencing individuals. From empowering Samson with great physical strength to helping the early Christians recall and record the teachings of Christ, the Holy Spirit has been instrumental in carrying out God's purposes.

Prayer: The Link to the Holy Spirit

One of the essential elements in a Christian's life is the act of prayer. It serves as a communication bridge, linking us directly with our Heavenly Father. In the context of Jesus' teaching in Luke 11:13, prayer emerges as a potent tool for seeking the Holy Spirit's guidance. If a believer genuinely longs to have the influence and guidance of the Holy Spirit in their life, they need to approach God in sincere, heartfelt prayer, asking for this spiritual aid.

Scripture also makes it clear that simply asking isn't enough. Our motives and the state of our heart play a significant role in the effectiveness of our prayers. James wrote, *"You ask and do not receive, because you ask with wrong motives, so that you may spend it on your passions"* (James 4:3, UASV). Therefore, it's crucial to approach God with a sincere heart, free from selfish motives when seeking the Holy Spirit.

The Early Christians: Models of Holy Spirit's Power

The Book of Acts provides us with numerous instances where early Christians demonstrated the impact of the Holy Spirit in their lives. Consider the day of Pentecost, where the apostles were able to speak in various tongues, not through their own abilities, but through the power of the Holy Spirit (Acts 2:4). The purpose was not for personal glory but to spread the good news of the kingdom of God.

Another enlightening instance is the case of Stephen, who, *"full of grace and power, was performing great wonders and signs among the people"* (Acts 6:8, UASV). Stephen's faith and reliance on God, coupled with the guidance of the Holy Spirit, empowered him to perform such wonders.

God's Generosity in Bestowing the Holy Spirit

As emphasized in Jesus' words, our Heavenly Father is more than willing to give us the spiritual help we seek. God's generosity is not to be taken lightly. Every good gift, every perfect present comes from Him (James 1:17). The Holy Spirit, which is a manifestation of God's active force, is among the greatest gifts one can receive. While it may not be given in overtly miraculous ways as it was during the early Christian congregation, its influence and guidance can still be felt in the life of a sincere believer.

The Apostle Paul reminds us in his letter to the Romans that the same power that resurrected Jesus is available to us (Romans 8:11). While he wasn't implying that the Holy Spirit dwells inside believers, the principle remains: the force that can raise the dead and transform lives is available to all who genuinely seek it.

Seeking the Holy Spirit with Persistence

It's also worth noting that while God is eager to give, our approach should be one of persistence. Jesus highlighted the importance of persistence in prayer through parables such as the persistent widow and the friend at midnight (Luke 18:1-8; Luke 11:5-13). These stories underscore the value of consistency and determination in our prayers. God values earnest seekers who are relentless in their pursuit of spiritual things.

A Personal Relationship with God

Our journey to benefit from the Holy Spirit begins with cultivating a deep personal relationship with God. Jesus emphasized the importance of this relationship when he said, *"This means eternal life, that they may know you, the only true God, and the one whom you sent, Jesus Christ"* (John 17:3, UASV). Our knowledge of God isn't merely academic. It is an intimate understanding, rooted in trust, love, and daily communion through prayer.

Faith as the Foundation

Merely asking isn't enough; our requests must be grounded in unwavering faith. The Apostle James wrote, *"But let him ask in faith, without doubting, for the one who doubts is like a wave of the sea driven and tossed by the wind"* (James 1:6, UASV). It is our faith, firm and unyielding, that acts as a foundation when we seek the Holy Spirit's guidance. Through faith, we confidently trust that God will respond to our earnest pleas and grant us the spiritual guidance we need.

Obedience and Conformity to God's Will

While faith is essential, it is equally crucial to align our lives with God's standards. The Scripture says, *"And whatever we ask we receive from Him, because we keep His commandments and do the things that are pleasing in His sight"* (1 John 3:22, UASV). This conformity to God's will serves as a testament to our genuine desire to be led by the Holy Spirit. God sees the heart, and when He finds one that is obedient and sincere, He is swift to grant the spiritual guidance sought.

The Lasting Benefits of the Holy Spirit's Guidance

The influence of the Holy Spirit in a believer's life goes beyond mere moments of insight or understanding. It molds our character, strengthens our resolve in the face of trials, and empowers us to live lives that are pleasing to God. The fruits of the Spirit, as described by the Apostle Paul, include love, joy, peace, patience, kindness, goodness, faithfulness, gentleness, and self-control (Galatians 5:22-23, UASV). With the Holy Spirit's guidance, these qualities can flourish within us, resulting in a life that is rich in spiritual blessings.

Drawing Closer to the End

As we draw closer to the conclusion of this chapter, let us be reminded of the profound gift that is available to us. In a world that often feels chaotic and uncertain, the steady guidance of the Holy Spirit can be our anchor. Through persistent prayer, unwavering faith, and obedience to God's commandments, we can experience the transformative power of the Holy Spirit in our lives.

In our subsequent journey as believers, let's strive to maintain a healthy prayer life, always seeking God's guidance. The Holy Spirit stands as a testament to God's immense love for us, eager to provide the necessary guidance and strength. By recognizing its value and earnestly seeking its influence, we fortify our spiritual walk, ensuring a life that glorifies God and reaps lasting spiritual benefits.

Conclusion

The power of the Holy Spirit is undeniable. Scripture provides countless examples of individuals who, under its influence, performed great deeds, exhibited unwavering faith, and bore witness to God's Kingdom. While the age of overt miracles has passed, the Holy Spirit's guidance remains available to all believers who genuinely seek it. By approaching our Heavenly Father in sincere, persistent prayer, and with a heart full of genuine motives, we can tap into this divine resource.

CHAPTER 4 The Father Provides Our Daily Needs

Introduction to God's Generosity

At the heart of our relationship with God is the profound truth that He deeply cares for His creation. This care isn't just in grand spiritual matters but also in our everyday needs. Jesus Christ, during His time on earth, drew attention to this aspect of God's nature, reinforcing the notion that if God looks after the smallest of His creations, how much more will He care for us, made in His image.

Understanding 'Daily Bread'

In the Lord's Prayer, Jesus taught us to pray: *"Give us each day our daily bread"* (Luke 11:3, UASV). This simple, yet profound request, touches on multiple layers of our existence. At its core, "daily bread" signifies sustenance and life. It represents our basic physical needs for survival, such as food and shelter. But delving deeper, it also symbolizes our spiritual nourishment, which we derive from Scripture and our relationship with God.

God's Care in Creation

One can see God's provision in the very fabric of creation. The world is designed with intricate systems that sustain life. From the life-giving water cycle to the crops that grow in their seasons, everything points to a Creator who has structured the earth to support the life that dwells upon it. As Isaiah 45:18 says, Jehovah *"formed the earth ... to be inhabited."* This designed habitability testifies to His desire and ability to cater to our physical needs.

Faith and Reliance on God's Provision

While it's clear that God has made provision for our needs, it's equally vital for believers to exercise faith and actively rely on Him. This faith isn't passive. It involves recognizing God as the ultimate source of our sustenance and seeking Him first in all things. Jesus, in His sermon on the mount, said, *"Seek first the kingdom of God and His righteousness, and all these things will be added to you"* (Matthew 6:33, UASV). This prioritization of spiritual matters doesn't negate our physical needs but places them in the correct perspective.

The Danger of Anxiety and the Assurance of Provision

In our fallen world, anxiety over daily needs is a common ailment. However, Jesus addressed this very concern. He pointed out that our Heavenly Father feeds the birds of the air and clothes the lilies of the field, neither of which toil nor spin. He then asks, *"Are you not of more value than they?"* (Matthew 6:26, UASV). This rhetorical question underscores a fundamental truth: if God takes care of these lesser creations, He will undoubtedly care for humanity, His prime creation.

The Spiritual 'Daily Bread'

While our physical needs are crucial, our spiritual needs are of paramount importance. Jesus once said, *"Man shall not live by bread alone, but by every word that proceeds out of the mouth of God"* (Matthew 4:4, UASV). This statement emphasizes the significance of spiritual sustenance, which we receive through God's Word. Just as our bodies require physical food for sustenance, our souls crave spiritual nourishment.

Scripture serves as this spiritual food. By meditating on it, studying it, and applying its teachings, we imbibe the spiritual nutrients that foster growth and maturity. This spiritual bread equips us to navigate the challenges of life, providing wisdom, guidance, and hope.

God's Provision in Times of Crisis

Scripture is replete with examples of God providing for His people, especially during times of crisis. Consider the Israelites in the wilderness. When they faced hunger, God rained down manna from heaven (Exodus 16). When they were thirsty, water sprang forth from a rock (Exodus 17). These instances weren't just about physical sustenance; they were demonstrations of God's steadfast love and commitment to His people.

Similarly, in today's world, many can testify to moments when, against all odds, their needs were met. These experiences serve to reinforce our faith, reminding us that our Father in heaven is actively involved in our lives.

Prayer as the Medium of Requesting Provision

Prayer remains the primary means by which we communicate our needs to God. It's through this divine communication channel that we humbly lay our requests before Him, expressing our dependence and trust in His provision. The Apostle Paul wrote, *"Let your requests be made known to God"* (Philippians 4:6, UASV). While God knows our needs even before we ask, the act of prayer is an expression of our reliance on Him.

Concluding Thoughts: Cultivating a Heart of Gratitude

Recognizing that all good things come from God should naturally foster a heart of gratitude. As we experience His provision, both physically and spiritually, it's essential to maintain an attitude of thanksgiving.

SECTION 2 IMPROVING OUR PRAYERS

Deepen your communication with God with "Improving Our Prayers." Explore how to foster a profound relationship with the Lord, integrate Scripture, cultivate gratitude, and benefit from communal prayer. Enhance the quality and depth of your prayers, drawing closer to the heart of God.

The act of prayer is one of the most fundamental practices in Christianity. For the believer, prayer is a lifeline to the Creator, a means of drawing close to God, seeking His wisdom, and finding comfort and guidance. As with any relationship, communication is vital to its health and growth. While there is no definitive "right" or "wrong" way to pray, we can strive to enhance the quality and depth of our communication with God.

Developing Intimacy with God

Fostering a Deep Relationship: At its heart, prayer is about cultivating a profound relationship with the Lord. Just as we grow close to friends by spending time with them and sharing our deepest thoughts, so too should our conversations with God evolve. Going beyond rote recitations or asking for blessings, we should seek to open our hearts fully, sharing our joys, fears, gratitude, and seeking His counsel in our lives.

Setting Aside Quiet Time: In today's bustling world, finding moments of peace can be a challenge. Yet, the quality of our prayers often improves when we designate specific times and places for quiet reflection and conversation with God. This not only minimizes distractions but also helps cultivate a discipline of daily communion with the Lord.

Seeking Alignment with God's Will

Praying with Purpose: God knows our hearts and our needs, but in praying, we affirm our dependence on Him. It's beneficial to be clear in our petitions, not because God needs specifics, but because it forces us to reflect on what we truly desire and need.

Submitting to His Will: While we may have our desires and requests, it's essential to remember Jesus' words in the Garden of Gethsemane: "not my will, but Yours be done." Recognizing and yielding to God's will, even if it differs from our own, reflects a mature and trusting relationship.

Using Scripture as a Foundation

Incorporating God's Word: The Bible isn't just a book; it's the inspired Word of God. By integrating Scripture into our prayers, we align ourselves with God's promises and commandments. It's a way to pray in agreement with God.

Memorizing and Reflecting: Committing Scripture to memory can aid our prayers. In moments of despair, joy, or confusion, these verses come to mind and guide our conversations with God, ensuring our prayers are rooted in truth and wisdom.

Cultivating a Heart of Gratitude

Beyond Petitions: While it's natural to approach God with our needs and concerns, prayers should not be solely a list of requests. We should also take time to thank Him for His blessings, express our love for Him, and simply worship His majesty.

Acknowledging All Circumstances: Paul encourages believers to "give thanks in all circumstances" (1 Thessalonians 5:18). Even in trials, there is room for gratitude, whether for God's presence, the growth we experience, or the hope of His promises.

The Role of Persistence and Patience

Ceaseless Prayer: Paul also tells us to "pray without ceasing" (1 Thessalonians 5:17). This doesn't mean we are to be in a constant state of formal prayer, but that we should maintain an ongoing dialogue with God, always attuned to His presence.

Trusting in His Timing: It can be disheartening when prayers seem unanswered. However, God operates beyond our understanding and timing. Continued prayer, even in the face of silence, is a testament to our faith and trust in God's perfect plan.

Community and Intercession

Praying with Others: While personal prayer is crucial, there's a unique power in communal prayer. Joining with others in supplication or thanksgiving fosters unity and often strengthens the fervency of our prayers.

Praying for Others: Intercession, or praying on behalf of others, is a powerful tool. It's a selfless act that aligns us with God's heart for all His children and reminds us of the broader body of Christ.

In conclusion, while God cherishes all sincere prayers, striving to enhance the depth and quality of our prayers can lead to a richer, more intimate relationship with Him. By aligning our hearts with Scripture, cultivating gratitude, practicing persistence, and praying in community, we can draw closer to the heart of God and find greater fulfillment and purpose in our spiritual lives.

CHAPTER 5 When Should We Pray?

The Power of Constant Communication

The very essence of prayer lies in its ability to bridge the gap between the mortal and the divine. As Christians navigate the challenges of life, they often question the appropriate times to approach God in prayer. Scripture, in its wisdom, doesn't confine prayer to certain hours or specific ceremonies. Instead, it paints a vivid picture of a God always eager to listen, implying that any moment can be the right moment.

The Biblical Encouragement to Pray Continuously

One of the most illuminating verses on the subject is found in the Apostle Paul's first letter to the Thessalonians. He wrote, *"Pray without ceasing"* (1 Thessalonians 5:17, UASV). This command doesn't necessarily mean being on one's knees every single moment but rather emphasizes maintaining an attitude of prayer, being in constant spiritual communion with God.

Scheduled Times of Prayer

Throughout biblical history, there have been set times where God's servants have approached Him in prayer. Daniel, for instance, had a practice of praying three times a day, facing Jerusalem from his Babylonian residence (Daniel 6:10). Such scheduled times of prayer can be beneficial, offering a structured approach to one's spiritual life.

They create moments in our day when we intentionally focus on God, pushing aside distractions to seek His face.

In Moments of Distress

Life is replete with trials and tribulations. In these moments of distress, turning to God in heartfelt prayer can bring comfort and guidance. King David, in many of his Psalms, exemplifies this approach. In times of danger, sorrow, or guilt, he would pour out his soul to God, seeking refuge and forgiveness. His words in Psalm 18:6 are poignant: *"In my distress I called upon Jehovah, and cried to my God"* (UASV).

Upon Waking and Before Sleep

The start and end of our day present unique opportunities for prayer. Morning prayers set the tone for the day, seeking God's guidance, protection, and wisdom. Evening prayers, on the other hand, are moments of reflection, gratitude for the day's blessings, and seeking forgiveness for any transgressions. Such practices help center our minds on spiritual matters, ensuring that God is the first and last thought of our day.

Before Meals

Expressing gratitude for our daily sustenance is a long-standing tradition among God's servants. Jesus himself set the example by giving thanks before meals (Matthew 15:36). Such moments remind us of God's provision, ensuring we never take His blessings for granted.

In Moments of Joy

While it's common to turn to God during hardships, it's equally crucial to approach Him in our moments of joy. The Apostle James wrote, *"Is anyone cheerful? Let him sing praises"* (James 5:13, UASV). By sharing our joy with God, we acknowledge Him as the source of all our blessings.

During Decision Making

Life presents us with countless decisions, from trivial daily choices to life-altering ones. In these moments, seeking God's wisdom and guidance through prayer is invaluable. Proverbs 3:5-6 reminds us to trust in Jehovah with all our heart and lean not on our understanding. By acknowledging Him in our decisions, He will make our paths straight.

Communal Prayer in Congregational Settings

While personal prayers are essential, there is also a place for communal prayers. When believers gather, their collective voice raised in supplication has a unique power. The early Christian congregation often engaged in such prayers, drawing strength from collective worship. In Acts 12, the church earnestly prayed for Peter's release from prison, a prayer that God miraculously answered.

Intercessory Prayers

Apart from personal needs, believers are encouraged to pray for others. Intercessory prayers, where one petitions on behalf of someone else, are a powerful way of showing love and concern. The Apostle Paul often requested such prayers and also prayed for the congregations he wrote to, showing the importance of this kind of supplication.

Conclusion: An Open Channel to God

The beauty of prayer lies in its accessibility. Jehovah God, the Creator of the universe, has made Himself available to listen to the cries, joys, fears, and hopes of His creation at any moment. While there are specific moments where prayer might seem especially apt, the reality is that any time is the right time.

Our journey as believers is enriched when we maintain a continuous line of communication with God. By recognizing the various moments we can approach Him, we ensure that our connection remains strong, our spiritual needs are met, and our relationship with our Heavenly Father continues to flourish.

CHAPTER 6 How Does God Communicate with Us Today?

The Necessity of Divine Communication

Our journey with God isn't a one-way street of us speaking to Him through prayer. It's a dynamic relationship where God also communicates with His servants. While the nature of this communication has evolved throughout biblical history, God's desire to guide, instruct, and comfort His people remains unchanging. In our present age, God's primary means of communication is through established channels that resonate with truth and clarity.

God's Word: The Bible as the Primary Channel

First and foremost, God communicates with us through His inspired Word, the Bible. This collection of books provides a comprehensive record of God's dealings with humanity, His expectations, promises, wisdom, and the profound truths about life and our purpose.

1. **Historical Accounts**: By studying the lives of individuals and nations in the Bible, we gain insights into God's character, His standards of righteousness, and His plan for humanity. The experiences of figures like Abraham, Moses, and David serve as lessons for us, offering both encouragement and caution.
2. **Prophetic Writings**: The prophets of old were direct mouthpieces of God. Their writings, filled with prophecies, exhortations, and divine messages, remain relevant, guiding us in understanding God's will and future promises.

3. **Wisdom Literature**: Books like Proverbs, Ecclesiastes, and Psalms provide a wealth of wisdom on leading a righteous life, handling challenges, and deepening our relationship with God.
4. **Apostolic Teachings**: The New Testament letters are foundational in understanding the teachings of Jesus Christ, the nature of the Christian congregation, and the hope for believers. They serve as guides in matters of doctrine, conduct, and spirituality.

Pastors and Spiritual Leaders

God, in His wisdom, has appointed individuals within the Christian congregation to shepherd and guide His flock. These pastors or spiritual leaders are entrusted with the task of teaching, correcting, and nourishing the believers under their care. When these leaders are grounded in Scripture and led by its principles, their teachings become a vital channel of God's communication. They can elucidate complex biblical concepts, offer counsel based on Scripture, and provide spiritual guidance.

Biblically Grounded Books and Lectures

We live in an age of information, where resources on biblical topics are vast. Biblically grounded books and lectures, written or delivered by well-informed Christian scholars and teachers, can be instrumental in deepening our understanding of God's Word. These resources can provide in-depth studies on specific topics, historical contexts, linguistic analyses, and doctrinal clarifications. When chosen discerningly, such books and lectures can enhance our appreciation of biblical truths and aid in our spiritual growth.

Principles over Prescriptions

While the Bible provides clear directives on certain matters, it often communicates through principles. Instead of explicit instructions for every situation, Scripture offers overarching principles that can be applied in various circumstances. This method allows believers to exercise personal judgment under the guidance of the Holy Spirit-inspired Word, ensuring their decisions align with God's will.

The Internal Witness of Scriptural Truth

There is an internal affirmation that occurs when one encounters scriptural truth. While we do not believe in the indwelling of the Holy Spirit, there's a resonance, a deep-seated affirmation within the believer when confronted with genuine biblical truth. This internal witness, grounded in our knowledge of Scripture and our relationship with God, serves as a compass, often confirming the authenticity of a message or doctrine.

The Role of Christian Fellowship

The Christian congregation isn't just a place of worship; it's a community where believers edify one another. Through fellowship, experiences are shared, testimonies are given, and scriptural insights are exchanged. In these interactions, God's guidance is often evident, as believers encourage and build one another up in the faith.

Conclusion: The Need for Discernment

In a world with numerous voices and interpretations, discernment becomes crucial in recognizing God's genuine communication channels. The Bereans were commended for examining the Scriptures daily to verify the Apostle Paul's teachings (Acts 17:11). In a similar vein, believers today must be like the Bereans, constantly weighing teachings and resources against the gold standard of the Bible.

By prioritizing the Bible, valuing biblically grounded spiritual leaders, and discerningly choosing resources, we ensure that our understanding of God's communication remains clear, pure, and untainted. Through these channels, God continues to guide, instruct, and communicate with His people, ensuring they walk in truth and righteousness.

CHAPTER 7 How Can We Improve Our Prayers?

The Essence of Prayer

Before diving into the ways we can enhance our prayers, it's pivotal to understand the very essence of prayer. At its core, prayer is a heartfelt communication with God, our Creator. It's a sacred conversation where we express our joys, sorrows, fears, desires, and gratitude. Just as any form of communication can benefit from refinement, so can our prayers. The goal isn't to make them more elaborate but to ensure they are sincere, effective, and aligned with God's will.

Approaching Prayer with Reverence

Jehovah is not just our Creator but the Sovereign of the universe. When we approach Him, it must be with the utmost reverence and respect. This doesn't imply an overly formal or rigid tone but an acknowledgment of His majesty and holiness. By starting our prayers with expressions of praise and adoration, we position our hearts rightly, recognizing who it is we are speaking to.

Scriptural Patterns in Prayer

The Bible offers a wealth of examples of prayer, providing models we can learn from. Consider the Lord's Prayer, where Jesus outlined a pattern, emphasizing key aspects that should be part of our supplications.

1. **Acknowledging God's Sovereignty**: *"Our Father in the heavens, let your name be sanctified"* (Matthew 6:9, UASV). Before

presenting personal requests, we acknowledge God's position and express the desire for His name to be revered.
2. **Seeking God's Will**: *"Let your kingdom come. Let your will take place, as in heaven, also on earth"* (Matthew 6:10, UASV). It's essential to prioritize God's purposes and will in our prayers.
3. **Presenting Personal Requests**: Jesus highlights asking for daily sustenance and forgiveness, indicating that personal requests have a place in our prayers (Matthew 6:11-12).

Clarity and Specificity

Vague prayers can often stem from vague thoughts. By being clear and specific in our requests, we not only express our desires more accurately but also position ourselves to recognize God's answers clearly. For instance, instead of merely praying for strength, one might ask for strength to overcome a specific temptation or challenge.

Praying in Line with God's Will

John wrote, *"And this is the confidence that we have before Him: that whenever we ask anything according to His will, He hears us"* (1 John 5:14, UASV). Our prayers must align with God's will. This requires immersion in Scripture, understanding God's purposes, principles, and promises. When our prayers align with His will, we can be confident they will be heard.

Avoiding Repetitious Prayers

Jesus warned against using *"vain repetitions"* in prayer (Matthew 6:7, UASV). While persistence in prayer is encouraged, mindless repetition isn't. Our prayers should be fresh, genuine expressions of our heart, not rote recitations.

Cultivating Humility

Our approach to Jehovah should always be with humility. Recognizing our imperfections and sinful nature, we approach God's throne of grace not based on our righteousness but on His mercy. Humility also entails acknowledging our dependence on Him for everything.

Including Prayers of Gratitude

While petitions are a significant component of our prayers, they shouldn't overshadow expressions of gratitude. Regularly reflecting on Jehovah's blessings and expressing genuine thankfulness enriches our prayer life.

The Role of Fasting

In certain situations, fasting while not obligatory can accompany our prayers to add intensity and express deep sincerity. While fasting, our physical abstention reflects a deeper spiritual yearning. It's not a way to 'twist God's arm' but rather a personal expression of earnestness.

The Impact of a Godly Lifestyle

How we live affects how we pray. The psalmist said, *"If I had cherished iniquity in my heart, Jehovah would not have listened"* (Psalm 66:18, UASV). Leading a life that aligns with Jehovah's standards enhances our confidence in approaching Him.

Improving Through Reflection and Practice

Like any form of communication, the more we pray, the better we become at it. Regular self-reflection, assessing the content, sincerity, and focus of our prayers, and making necessary adjustments, can significantly improve our prayer life.

Conclusion: A Lifelong Journey of Growth

Improving our prayers isn't about achieving perfection but about deepening our relationship with God. As we grow in our Christian walk, our prayers will reflect this growth. By continually seeking to refine our prayers, we ensure that our communication with our Heavenly Father remains vibrant, sincere, and effective.

CHAPTER 8 Why Does God Reject Some Prayers

The Complex Nature of Unanswered Prayers

The subject of unanswered prayers is one that perplexes many Christians. If God is an all-powerful and loving God, why would He reject some prayers? Addressing this issue requires careful examination of Scriptural truths and the principles that govern divine communication. Understanding why some prayers go unanswered can not only deepen our relationship with God but also refine the quality and effectiveness of our prayers.

God's Sovereign Will: The Ultimate Standard

First and foremost, we must acknowledge God as the sovereign ruler of the universe. His will is perfect and aligns with His nature, wisdom, and ultimate purposes for humanity and the cosmos. As much as He desires to bless us, God will never act in a way that contradicts His will. James 4:3 highlights the problem of asking with wrong motives: *"You ask and do not receive because you ask wrongly, so you can spend it on your passions"* (James 4:3, UASV). A prayer that is out of sync with God's will is not one that He can honor.

Prayer as Alignment, Not Just Request

Prayer isn't merely a list of requests presented to God; it is also an act of aligning our will with His. Jesus exemplified this perfectly in His prayer at Gethsemane, saying, *"Not my will, but yours, be done"* (Luke

22:42, UASV). If our prayers are more about our will than God's, then we've misunderstood the fundamental essence of prayer.

The Impact of Sin and Disobedience

The Scriptures make it evident that Jehovah is holy and cannot look favorably upon sin. In Isaiah 59:2, we read: *"But your iniquities have made a separation between you and your God, and your sins have hidden His face from you, so that He does not hear"* (Isaiah 59:2, UASV). A life of willful sin and disobedience can be a severe barrier to effective prayer.

Lack of Faith: A Critical Barrier

Faith is an indispensable component in the life of a believer and inherently affects the quality of our prayers. James says, *"But he must ask in faith without doubting, for the one who doubts is like a wave of the sea, driven and tossed by the wind"* (James 1:6, UASV). A lack of faith can make our prayers ineffective and may result in their being rejected by God.

Wrong Motives and Selfish Desires

Our motives in prayer are crucial. God examines the heart and understands our deepest thoughts and intentions. If we approach Him with selfish motives, seeking only to satisfy our desires, our prayers may go unanswered. As we've seen earlier, James 4:3 directly addresses this issue. Selfishness in prayer is a stark contrast to the humility and sincerity that should characterize our approach to Jehovah.

The Role of Persistence in Prayer

Some prayers may seem unanswered because they require persistent asking on our part. The Parable of the Persistent Widow in Luke 18:1-8 underscores the importance of continual, fervent prayer. However, persistence should not be confused with mere repetition or insistence that leans towards a demand. The former reflects a deep-seated trust in Jehovah's timing, while the latter implies an attitude of entitlement or impatience.

Interpersonal Relationships and Unanswered Prayers

The quality of our interpersonal relationships, particularly within the family unit, can influence the effectiveness of our prayers. Peter warns husbands to dwell with their wives *"according to knowledge,"* so that their prayers may not be hindered (1 Peter 3:7, UASV). A failure to maintain godly relationships may result in our prayers being impeded or rejected.

Not Recognizing the Answer

At times, God answers our prayers in ways that are not immediately obvious to us. His answer may be "no," "wait," or provide an alternative that we had not considered. Our limited human perspective may fail to recognize God's answers, leading us to wrongly assume that our prayers have been rejected.

The Spiritual Dichotomy of Divine Distance and Nearness: An Exegetical Examination of Proverbs 15:29

Proverbs 15:29 (UASV)

²⁹ Jehovah is far from the wicked,
but the prayer of the righteous he hears.

"Jehovah is far from the wicked"

- *The Lord*: Jehovah, the one true God of Israel, who stands as the sovereign ruler of the universe.

- *is far from*: The phrase suggests not mere geographical distance but moral and spiritual separation. God is portrayed as remote or disconnected from individuals who engage in wicked activities.

- *the wicked*: These are individuals who knowingly defy God's moral and ethical standards, choosing to live in ways that are contrary to His will.

This first clause drives home the idea that wickedness results in a form of separation from Jehovah. It is not that He is unaware of them; rather, His moral character necessitates that He distances Himself from those who choose to walk in wickedness.

"but the prayer of the righteous he hears"

- *but*: This conjunction sets up a contrast between the fate of the wicked and the privileged position of the righteous.
- *the prayer*: The specific channel through which the righteous communicate with God, highlighting the importance of prayer in maintaining a close relationship with Him.
- *of the righteous*: These are the individuals who earnestly strive to live in alignment with God's laws and principles.
- *he hears*: The verb "hears" in this context signifies more than auditory perception; it implies attentiveness, consideration, and action. Jehovah doesn't just hear; He listens with intent to act favorably.

The latter part of the verse highlights the proximity of Jehovah to those who live righteously. Not only is He near them, but He is also actively involved in their lives, attentive to their prayers.

In summary, Proverbs 15:29 portrays a clear spiritual dichotomy: Jehovah maintains a distance from the wicked, while drawing near to the righteous, especially through the medium of prayer. This verse serves as a poignant reminder of the tangible benefits of righteous living and the spiritual consequences of turning away from God's ways.

The Futility of Prayer Without Obedience: A Detailed Analysis of Proverbs 28:9

"If one turns away his ear from hearing the law"

- *If*: This conditional word immediately indicates that what follows is contingent upon a particular action or choice.
- *one turns away his ear*: A metaphorical expression that describes intentional disregard or willful ignorance. It is an active choice

to ignore, which is far more egregious than mere forgetfulness or misunderstanding.

- *from hearing the law*: Here, "the law" refers to the divinely given Torah or the general principles of God's righteousness and moral imperatives.

This first clause puts forth a scenario where someone consciously chooses to ignore God's teachings. They "turn away" from it, indicating that at some point, they had access to it or even may have engaged with it, but have now decided to ignore its guidance.

"even his prayer is detestable"

- *even*: This word serves as an amplifier to drive home the gravity of the situation. It adds a sense of weight to what is being said next.

- *his prayer*: Refers to the act of communicating with God, which is generally considered a sacred and meaningful act.

- *is detestable*: A strong term indicating not just disfavor but a level of revulsion or disgust. The Hebrew term carries connotations of abomination.

The second clause then delivers a powerful and challenging statement: ignoring God's law renders even one's prayers, which should be a means of intimate communication with God, as something "detestable" to God. The point is clear: prayer is not just about uttering words, but it needs to be backed by a life committed to obeying God's law.

Conclusion: Towards a More Discerning Prayer Life

Understanding why Jehovah may reject some prayers offers a valuable pathway to refining our prayer life. It invites introspection, spurs us to align our will with Jehovah's, and challenges us to approach our Creator with humility, reverence, and a sincere heart. Unanswered prayers are not a cue for disillusionment but an opportunity for spiritual growth and deeper understanding of God's divine nature and perfect will.

SECTION 3 PRAYERS THAT THE FATHER LISTENS TO AND ANSWERS IF THEY ARE ACCORDING TO HIS WILL AND PURPOSES

Uncover the power of prayers aligned with God's will and purposes. Learn how a deep-rooted understanding of God's character, coupled with faith-filled petitions, can lead to prayers that the Father not only listens to but answers. Discover the transformative power of a prayer life in harmony with the heart of God.

Prayer is one of the most profound ways in which we communicate with our Creator. Yet, not all prayers receive the answer we might anticipate. Scripture makes it clear that there are certain prayers that the Father is particularly attentive to—those that align with His will and purposes. Such prayers resonate with the heart of God and play a role in the unfolding of His divine plan.

Harmony with God's Word

One of the key aspects of a prayer that is in line with God's will is its harmony with Scripture. The Bible provides us with a comprehensive understanding of God's character, desires, and plans for humanity. When our prayers reflect the truths found in Scripture, they are more likely to be in sync with His will.

James 4:3 states, "You ask and do not receive, because you ask wrongly, to spend it on your passions." This highlights the importance of ensuring our prayers are not rooted in selfish desires but rather in the broader perspective of God's plan and purposes.

Praying in Jesus' Name

Another fundamental element in prayers that align with the Father's will is the act of praying in the name of Jesus. This is not simply a ritualistic phrase, but a profound recognition of the authority and role of Jesus in our prayers. When we pray in His name, we are effectively approaching God on the basis of Christ's merit and righteousness, not our own.

John 14:13-14 says, "Whatever you ask in my name, this I will do, that the Father may be glorified in the Son. If you ask me anything in my name, I will do it." This Scripture emphasizes the importance and power of invoking Jesus' name in our petitions.

Surrender to God's Sovereignty

A prayer aligned with God's will often includes an element of surrender. Instead of dictating to God what we believe should happen, it acknowledges His sovereignty and supreme wisdom. A heartfelt, "Not my will, but Yours be done," mirrors Jesus' own prayer in the Garden of Gethsemane (*Luke 22:42*).

This surrender doesn't signify resignation or apathy. Rather, it reflects a deep trust in God's goodness and His overarching plan, even when circumstances appear challenging or unclear.

Interceding for Others

Intercessory prayer is a powerful way we can align our prayers with God's will. When we lift up others, praying for their well-being, salvation, or specific needs, we participate in God's desire to bless and heal His creation. Paul's letters are filled with examples of intercessory prayers, and he often exhorts believers to pray for one another.

1 Timothy 2:1-4 urges, "First of all, then, I urge that supplications, prayers, intercessions, and thanksgivings be made for all people… This is good, and it is pleasing in the sight of God our Savior, who desires all people to be saved and to come to the knowledge of the truth."

The Role of the Holy Spirit

The Holy Spirit plays an indispensable role in guiding our prayers. Romans 8:26 tells us that "the Spirit helps us in our weakness. For we do not know what to pray for as we ought, but the Spirit himself intercedes for us with groanings too deep for words." By being receptive to the Holy Spirit's promptings, we can pray with greater discernment and alignment with God's will.

Praying with Perseverance

Consistency and persistence in prayer, even when answers seem delayed, demonstrates faith and trust in God's timing and wisdom. Jesus Himself encouraged persistent prayer in parables like the persistent widow (*Luke 18:1-8*). Such perseverance shows our commitment to seeking God's will, even when the path is not immediately clear.

A healthy prayer life involves more than presenting our list of wants and needs to God. It requires a deep-rooted desire to seek God's will and purposes. By grounding our prayers in Scripture, praying in Jesus' name, surrendering to God's sovereignty, interceding for others, being guided by the Holy Spirit, and persisting in our petitions, we position ourselves in a posture of humility and alignment with God's heart.

The Heart's Posture in Prayer

At the very core of prayers that God listens to is the posture of our hearts. Approaching God with sincerity, humility, and a genuine desire to hear from Him makes our prayers powerful. God looks at the heart behind the prayer more than the eloquence of words. *1 Samuel*

16:7 reminds us, "For the Lord sees not as man sees: man looks on the outward appearance, but the Lord looks on the heart."

Faith-Filled Prayers

Hebrews 11:6 tells us that "without faith it is impossible to please Him, for whoever would draw near to God must believe that He exists and that He rewards those who seek Him." Our faith is a crucial component in our prayers. When we come to God genuinely believing that He can and will act according to His good purposes, our prayers resonate with the Father's heart.

Alignment with God's Character

Understanding God's character is vital. The more we know who God is — His love, justice, mercy, sovereignty, and goodness — the more our prayers will align with His nature. As we spend time in His Word and grow in our knowledge of Him, our prayers will naturally shift towards His desires and purposes.

Being Open to God's Response

Finally, being receptive to how God might respond is crucial. Sometimes His answers may come in unexpected ways or at unexpected times. Sometimes He might say "yes," other times "no," or "wait." Regardless of the response, trust that God, in His infinite wisdom, knows what's best. *Isaiah 55:8-9* states, "For my thoughts are not your thoughts, neither are your ways my ways, declares God. For as the heavens are higher than the earth, so are my ways higher than your ways and my thoughts than your thoughts."

In Closing

The essence of effective prayer isn't about getting what we want, but about aligning our desires with those of our Heavenly Father. As we grow in our understanding of Him, His Word, and His purposes, our prayers will naturally align more closely with His heart. The promise remains: when we call out to God, especially in ways that resonate with His divine will and purposes, He hears, and He answers.

CHAPTER 9 The Father Listens to the Prayer of the Humble and the Contrite

Introduction: The Essence of Godly Character in Prayer

Prayer remains one of the most personal and profound ways we communicate with our Heavenly Father. While Jehovah is open to hearing the petitions and pleas of all His children, Scripture makes it abundantly clear that certain dispositions resonate more deeply with the heart of God. Among these are humility and contrition. Exploring these twin virtues in the context of prayer not only opens up profound Scriptural insights but also affords believers a more effective and enriching prayer life.

Humility: The Bedrock of Effective Prayer

The Bible continually extols the virtue of humility in the life of a believer. In fact, it is a quality that Jehovah Himself values highly. In the Book of Proverbs, we are told that *"Haughty eyes and a proud heart, the lamp of the wicked, are sin!"* (Proverbs 21:4, UASV). Conversely, Proverbs 3:34 makes it evident that *"He mocks the mockers, but He gives grace to the humble"* (UASV). The humble disposition is like fertile ground where the seeds of effective prayer can grow and flourish.

The Humility of Christ: The Ultimate Model

The most sterling example of humility we have is in Jesus Christ. The Apostle Paul encourages believers to have the same mindset as Christ, who, despite being in the form of God, *"did not regard equality with God something to be grasped, but emptied himself by taking the form of a slave"* (Philippians 2:6-7, UASV). If the Son of God, who had every reason to assert His divinity, chose instead the path of humility, how much more should we, as imperfect beings, approach Jehovah with humble hearts?

Contrition: A Spirit Broken yet Receptive

Contrition, or a broken spirit, does not imply a sense of hopelessness or despair. Rather, it indicates a heart that recognizes its own limitations and sins, yet turns towards Jehovah for forgiveness and guidance. King David epitomizes a contrite spirit in Psalm 51 when he pleads for God's mercy following his sin with Bathsheba. David writes, *"The sacrifices of God are a broken spirit; A broken and a contrite heart, O God, You will not despise"* (Psalm 51:17, UASV).

The Theology of Grace: Undeserved Kindness Meets Humility and Contrition

Grace and humility are interwoven in the fabric of Christian theology. Ephesians 2:8-9 states, *"For by grace you have been saved through faith; and this is not of yourselves, it is the gift of God; it is not of works, so that no one may boast"* (UASV). The recognition that we are saved by grace alone should drive us to our knees in humility and contrition, aware that we can claim no merit of our own.

The Dynamics of Prayer: Engaging God with Humility and Contrition

How does one practically engage in prayer characterized by humility and contrition? Firstly, by acknowledging God's sovereignty and our utter dependence on Him. Secondly, by confessing our sins honestly and specifically, never presuming upon God's grace. Thirdly, by voicing our petitions and intercessions without entitlement, knowing that even our best deeds are but filthy rags in the sight of an infinitely holy God. And finally, by expressing gratitude for His enduring love and mercy, attributing all good things in our lives to His benevolent hand.

Divine Reception: God's Proactive Response to Humble and Contrite Prayers

Jehovah doesn't merely passively listen to the humble and contrite. Scripture makes it clear that God actively draws near to such individuals. The Prophet Isaiah relays God's words when he writes, *"For this is what the high and lofty One says, Who resides forever, whose name is holy: 'I dwell in the high and holy place, but also with the contrite and humble in spirit, to revive the spirit of the humble, and to revive the heart of the contrite'"* (Isaiah 57:15, UASV). There is divine receptivity, and even proactive grace, towards those who approach God in humility and contrition.

The True Sacrifice: Understanding the Depth of Psalm 51:17

"The sacrifices of God are a broken spirit"
- *The sacrifices of God*: The term "sacrifices" here doesn't refer to animal sacrifices or ritualistic offerings but rather to what God truly values in devotion.

- *are*: The verb establishes not a suggestion but a factual condition about what God desires.
- *a broken spirit*: The term "broken" doesn't imply defeat but rather humility and surrender. "Spirit" refers to one's inner being or disposition.

This first part of the verse emphatically states that what God really values is not ritualistic compliance but a spirit that is humble and fully surrendered to Him.

"a broken and contrite heart, O God, you will not despise"

- *a broken and contrite heart*: Similar to "a broken spirit," this phrase emphasizes the disposition God values. "Contrite" means feeling or showing sorrow for one's sins.
- *O God*: Direct address to God, indicating that the psalmist is not just stating a fact but is in a conversation with the Divine.
- *you will not despise*: Strong affirmation that God will not reject or look down upon such a heart.

The second clause serves as both affirmation and promise. It declares God's stance toward those who approach Him with genuine humility and repentance.

In summary, Psalm 51:17 shifts the focus away from external acts of worship to the internal condition of the worshiper. It affirms that God values a humble spirit and a repentant heart over ritualistic sacrifices. This serves as a profound reminder that the state of our hearts is paramount in our relationship with God.

The Divine Healer of Emotional and Physical Afflictions: An Exposition on Psalm 147:3

"He heals the brokenhearted"

"He heals": The verb "heals" immediately identifies Jehovah as the ultimate source of all healing. While human doctors may attend to physical ailments, Jehovah operates in a realm beyond the capabilities of human medicine. The term "heals" doesn't merely imply a temporary fix but indicates a thorough restoration to the original condition. This phrase aligns with the objective Historical-Grammatical method of interpretation, emphasizing that Jehovah's healing is both actual and practical, not allegorical or symbolic.

"the brokenhearted": This term signifies those who are emotionally and spiritually shattered. Life's trials, disappointments, and tragedies can leave people brokenhearted, but Jehovah's comfort and assurances can heal even these profound emotional wounds. Unlike human efforts that may offer temporary relief, Jehovah's healing targets the underlying issues, offering hope and strength. While some may argue that the term "brokenhearted" could symbolize something different, in the scope of a literal interpretation, it clearly refers to those suffering emotional distress.

"And binds up their wounds."

"and binds up": This part of the verse introduces a parallel action to the healing. To "bind up" signifies a hands-on, personal care, much like a physician who meticulously dresses a wound. The term is active and ongoing, emphasizing that Jehovah's care is both immediate and sustaining. It is not a one-time act but an enduring promise of maintenance and preservation.

"their wounds": The reference to "wounds" serves as a specific example of what Jehovah heals, and it expands the range of His healing to include not just emotional but also physical afflictions. This phrase reinforces that Jehovah's care extends to all aspects of human suffering, be it emotional or physical.

In sum, Psalm 147:3 serves as a comforting reassurance of Jehovah's active role as the healer of both emotional and physical wounds. It is a verse rich in its literal meaning, emphasizing Jehovah's comprehensive care for the suffering. It supports the view that God allows suffering but is also the ultimate source of healing, without resorting to allegorical interpretations.

Edward D. Andrews

Jehovah's Attentive Ear and Delivering Hand: An Exposition on Psalm 34:17

"The righteous cry, and Jehovah hears"

"The righteous cry": The term "righteous" here refers to those who are in a right standing with Jehovah, adhering to His moral and ethical standards. The act of "crying" implies a fervent calling out or praying, signifying moments of distress or need. It's worth noting that the text specifies that the righteous, not just anyone, are heard by Jehovah, making clear that there is a moral component to divine attention.

"and Jehovah hears": The conjunction "and" serves to immediately link the act of crying out to Jehovah's response, offering a swift assurance that the call does not go unanswered. The verb "hears" is significant, emphasizing Jehovah's attentiveness to the pleas of the righteous. This listening is not passive but active, indicating a readiness to respond. Jehovah isn't a distant God but is actively involved in the lives of those who seek to live according to His standards.

"And delivers them out of all their troubles."

"and delivers them": The action moves from hearing to delivering, demonstrating that Jehovah's attention results in tangible intervention. The term "delivers" is a strong word that implies a complete rescue or setting free from a form of bondage or suffering. Jehovah's deliverance is effective and comprehensive; it is not partial or incomplete.

"out of all their troubles": This phrase expands on the scope of Jehovah's deliverance. It is not limited to certain kinds of difficulties but includes "all" troubles. It underscores Jehovah's omnipotence and his comprehensive care for the righteous. While the extent and timing of this deliverance can vary, the promise remains steadfast: Jehovah's help is all-encompassing and not restricted by the magnitude or complexity of the problem.

In summary, Psalm 34:17 paints a vivid picture of Jehovah as an attentive listener and an effective deliverer for those who are in a right relationship with Him. Through a literal, Historical-Grammatical lens, this verse strongly supports the idea that while God allows suffering, He is also the ultimate source of deliverance for the righteous, without the need for allegorical interpretation.

The Contrast Between Wicked Sacrifices and Upright Prayers: An Exposition on Proverbs 15:8

"The sacrifice of the wicked is detestable to Jehovah."

"The sacrifice of the wicked": The term "sacrifice" generally denotes a ritualistic offering meant to honor God. However, when it is said to be "of the wicked," the efficacy and acceptability of such a sacrifice are immediately called into question. The "wicked" refers to those who live in opposition to Jehovah's moral and ethical standards. Such sacrifices are mere rituals devoid of genuine faith or righteousness.

"is detestable to Jehovah": The term "detestable" is powerful, indicating a strong form of repulsion. This underscores the severity of how Jehovah views empty rituals when performed by individuals who are not living in accord with His requirements. It emphasizes the importance Jehovah places on the heart condition and moral standing of the one offering the sacrifice, rather than the act itself.

"But the prayer of the upright is his delight."

"but the prayer": The conjunction "but" serves as a pivotal turning point in the verse, introducing a contrast that is both stark and instructive. It shifts the focus from ritualistic actions to sincere communication with Jehovah. The term "prayer" is used to represent an act of pure spiritual devotion, devoid of any superficial rituals.

"of the upright": The "upright" refers to those who walk in integrity and righteousness, aligning their lives with Jehovah's standards. Unlike the wicked, their lives are in harmony with their prayers, lending credibility and weight to their petitions before Jehovah.

"is his delight": The word "delight" here is antithetical to "detestable," showing how Jehovah finds joy and pleasure in the prayers of the upright. It indicates that not only are these prayers heard, but they are also welcomed and cherished by Jehovah. This reveals the deep emotional resonance that the prayers of the upright have with Jehovah, affirming His loving and relational nature.

In conclusion, Proverbs 15:8 sharply contrasts the worthlessness of empty rituals performed by the wicked with the preciousness of sincere prayers offered by the upright. Analyzed through a literal, Historical-Grammatical lens, this verse offers a nuanced understanding of what is truly valuable to Jehovah, stressing the importance of integrity and righteousness in one's relationship with Him.

Conclusion: A Call to Cultivate Humility and Contrition in Our Prayer Lives

The virtues of humility and contrition are not optional add-ons to the Christian experience; they are fundamental traits that Jehovah expects to find in His children. In a world increasingly obsessed with self-aggrandizement and pride, the humble and contrite heart stands as a powerful testimony to the transformative work of the Holy Spirit. As we seek to deepen our relationship with Jehovah through prayer, let us diligently cultivate these qualities, assured that our Father not only hears but delights in such prayers.

CHAPTER 10 The Eyes of the Father Are Toward the Righteous and Their Cry

Introduction: The Ever-Watchful Eyes of Jehovah

The concept of God's watchfulness over His creation is both comforting and awe-inspiring. But what is even more touching is the Scriptural assertion that His eyes are specifically "toward the righteous" and that He hears "their cry" (Psalm 34:15, UASV). This chapter aims to delve into the profound implications of this truth and to guide believers on how they can position themselves under the caring gaze and attentive ear of our Heavenly Father.

The Righteous: Defined by Scripture, Not Human Standards

Before we proceed, it's imperative to clarify what the term "righteous" means in a Scriptural context. Contrary to cultural misconceptions, righteousness is not a status achieved by human effort or moral superiority. Rather, it is a state of being in right standing with God, made possible only through faith in Jesus Christ. "For by works of the law no human being will be justified in his sight, since through the law comes knowledge of sin" (Romans 3:20, UASV). True righteousness is a divine endowment, not a human accomplishment.

The Focused Gaze of Jehovah: Not a Passive Observation

Understanding that Jehovah's eyes are upon the righteous is not to suggest some passive, distant observation. The original language and cultural background indicate a direct, purposeful, and active gaze. Jehovah's watchfulness implies His ongoing, personal involvement in the lives of His children. He's not merely a spectator; He's a proactive Father engaged in every facet of their lives.

The Connection Between Righteousness and Prayer

So, how does this focused gaze relate to our prayer lives? The Apostle James gives us a clue when he writes, "The prayer of a righteous person is very powerful in its effect" (James 5:16, UASV). A person who is in right standing with God, who walks in obedience to His commands and is sensitive to His will, offers prayers that are both powerful and effective. Therefore, righteousness becomes a critical factor in the efficacy of our prayers.

The Cry of the Righteous: A Symphony of Desperation and Trust

The cry of the righteous is not a mere utterance of words. It is a heartfelt plea, an expression of genuine need backed by trust in Jehovah's providence. This kind of "cry" transcends mere words; it's an anguished soul reaching out to its Creator in desperation, confident that He will hear and respond. The cry of the righteous is not an expression of doubt but a manifestation of deep faith and reliance on Jehovah.

How Does Jehovah Respond to the Cry of the Righteous?

Scripture affords us numerous examples of how God responds to the righteous cry. One compelling illustration is the story of Hannah, who was childless and deeply distressed. She poured out her soul to Jehovah in earnest prayer, and God granted her request for a son (1 Samuel 1:9-20). Here, Jehovah not only heard Hannah's cry but took action in line with her request, showcasing His proactive responsiveness to the cry of the righteous.

Jehovah's Watchfulness as a Safeguard Against Adversity

Jehovah's watchfulness also serves as a divine safeguard against the pitfalls and adversities that might befall the righteous. Proverbs 10:3 states, "Jehovah will not let the soul of the righteous go hungry, but he thrusts away the craving of the wicked" (UASV). Being under Jehovah's watchful eye assures protection and provision, making it an indispensable aspect of the prayer lives of believers.

Implications for Our Prayer Life: The Role of Righteousness

So what are the practical implications of all this for our prayer lives? Being aware that Jehovah's eyes are toward the righteous should serve as an incentive to maintain a godly lifestyle. It should steer us away from sin, drive us to continual repentance, and inspire us to walk faithfully with Jehovah. This righteousness not only pleases Jehovah but also amplifies the power and effectiveness of our prayers.

Jehovah's Attentive Watchfulness and Receptive Listening: An Exposition on Psalm 34:15

"The eyes of Jehovah are toward the righteous."

"The eyes of Jehovah": The phrase "the eyes of Jehovah" symbolizes divine attentiveness. While anthropomorphic in language, the implication is clear: Jehovah is not an impersonal or detached deity but is intimately concerned with human affairs. These "eyes" are directed towards specific individuals, indicating a focused form of attention.

"are toward the righteous": The direction of Jehovah's gaze is crucial—He is watching "the righteous." As established in other texts, righteousness is not a matter of ritual compliance but involves a life aligned with Jehovah's moral and ethical requirements. This reaffirms the notion that Jehovah's attention is selective based on moral and spiritual criteria.

"And his ears toward their cry."

"and his ears": This transition moves from the visual aspect of God's awareness to the auditory, indicating a full-sensory attentiveness. It amplifies the notion that Jehovah is not just a watcher but also a listener. This dual sensory expression enhances the understanding that Jehovah is intimately connected with His worshippers in multiple dimensions.

"toward their cry": Jehovah's ears are not attuned to idle chatter or empty ritualistic words, but to the "cry" of the righteous. This "cry" can be understood as earnest prayers, calls for help, or even unarticulated emotional yearnings. It implies a sense of urgency and sincerity, qualities that Jehovah values.

In sum, Psalm 34:15 succinctly captures Jehovah's intimate attentiveness to the righteous, both in what He sees and hears. Through a literal, Historical-Grammatical lens, this verse complements the understanding that Jehovah is not a distant deity but is closely involved in the lives of those who seek to align themselves with His will. His watchfulness and receptiveness underscore His readiness to act in favor of the righteous, affirming that while suffering is a part of the human experience, Jehovah is neither indifferent nor unresponsive.

Conclusion: Living and Praying under the Divine Gaze

Understanding that the eyes of Jehovah are toward the righteous and that He hears their cry is a powerful reality that should profoundly impact our approach to prayer. It offers both a comfort and a challenge: comfort in knowing that we are continually under the loving gaze and attentive ear of our Heavenly Father, and a challenge to live a life worthy of this divine attention. As we seek to enrich our prayer lives, may we strive to be righteous in God's eyes, fully aware that such a stance enables our prayers to be both powerful and effective.

CHAPTER 11 The Power of Prayer—Not All Requests Are Granted

Introduction: The Paradox of Unanswered Prayers

A powerful, but often misunderstood, facet of prayer is that not all requests are granted, even when they come from devout believers. This is not a flaw in the system of divine interaction but rather an integral part of the complex relationship between the Creator and His creation. This chapter aims to demystify the reasons behind this phenomenon, explaining why some prayers go unanswered or yield an outcome different from what was sought.

The Omnipotence of Jehovah and the Limits of Human Understanding

Let's first acknowledge the omnipotence of Jehovah, the Creator of the universe. His power is beyond human comprehension, and His wisdom transcends our understanding. Isaiah 55:9 reminds us that "as the heavens are higher than the earth, so are my ways higher than your ways and my thoughts than your thoughts" (UASV). God can do anything within the parameters of His character, but this does not mean He will grant every human request.

Alignment with God's Will: The Primordial Factor

The most vital aspect to consider in unanswered prayers is whether the request aligns with Jehovah's will. Jesus Himself provided the perfect example in the Garden of Gethsemane. Facing imminent arrest and crucifixion, Jesus prayed earnestly for the cup to pass from Him. Yet, His ultimate desire was not His comfort but the fulfillment of God's will. He added, "not as I will, but as you will" (Matthew 26:39, UASV). Jesus's prayer teaches us that our will should always be secondary to Jehovah's.

The Role of Right Timing

Sometimes, the issue is not what we ask for but when we ask for it. Jehovah operates according to His perfect timing, not ours. Just as the prophet Habakkuk was told, "For the vision is yet for the appointed time ... Though it delays, wait for it" (Habakkuk 2:3, UASV), so too our prayers may require a waiting period aligned with God's divine timing.

The Building Blocks of Character: Lessons Through Denial

Often, unanswered prayers serve as building blocks of character. God uses these situations to cultivate virtues such as patience, resilience, and trust in His divine judgment. The Apostle Paul's plea for relief from his "thorn in the flesh" was met with a response that God's grace was sufficient for him (2 Corinthians 12:7-9, UASV). Sometimes, God's 'No' is a 'Yes' to something more significant in character development and spiritual maturation.

Contradictions in the Petitions: When Our Prayers Collide

At times, unanswered prayers result from the contradictory nature of multiple prayers. For instance, two students praying to top the same class or athletes praying to win the same championship cannot both have their prayers answered affirmatively. In such cases, Jehovah exercises His wisdom to decide which request aligns best with His broader purposes.

The Danger of Presumptuous Prayers

Presumptuous prayers are those that impose our will upon God, without due consideration for His divine plan. James 4:3 warns, "You ask and do not receive because you ask wrongly, to spend it on your passions" (UASV). Such prayers stem from selfish motives and are unlikely to receive Jehovah's approval. Therefore, it's crucial to examine the intentions behind our petitions constantly.

Jehovah's Silence: Absence of an Immediate Answer is Not Absence of Action

It is crucial to distinguish between Jehovah's silence and His rejection. A lack of immediate answer does not signify God's indifference or lack of power. Often, He is working behind the scenes in ways we cannot comprehend. Like a skilled craftsman, Jehovah doesn't rush His work but takes His time to accomplish His purposes perfectly, even when it involves answering our prayers.

Practical Tips for Handling Unanswered Prayers

The appropriate response to unanswered prayers is not disillusionment but a resolute faith in Jehovah's wisdom. Such situations are opportunities to delve deeper into prayer and Scripture, seeking to align our will more closely with God's. They are also moments to consult spiritually mature individuals for guidance and perspective.

The Bounds of Prayer in Jesus' Name: An Exegesis on John 14:13-14

"Whatever you ask in my name": The phrase "in my name" is central to understanding the condition under which the prayers are answered. This isn't a "magic phrase" to be tacked on to any request. Rather, asking "in Jesus' name" entails praying in harmony with His character, will, and purpose. It is not carte blanche for any request.

"this I will do": At first glance, this might seem like an unconditional promise to fulfill any request, but the context and the condition ("in my name") inherently limit it. Jesus will act if the request aligns with His will and the Father's overarching plans.

"so that the Father may be glorified in the Son": This clause provides the ultimate objective of answered prayers—to bring glory to the Father through the Son. It serves as a litmus test for the type of prayers that will be answered. Prayers that do not align with this aim are unlikely to be granted.

"If you ask me anything in my name": This repetition in verse 14 reinforces the conditional nature of the promise and serves to emphasize its importance. Again, it is not an open invitation to ask for anything indiscriminately but has the qualification of being "in Jesus' name"—aligned with His will and character.

"I will do it": Similar to the first verse, this reiteration serves to underscore the reliability of Jesus in answering prayers that meet the stated conditions. It offers assurance while subtly reminding the audience of the limitations set forth.

In summary, John 14:13-14 is not a blank check for believers to make any demands they see fit. It is often misunderstood and abused by those who perceive God as a sort of cosmic genie. The verses establish the criteria for effective prayer—asking in accordance with Jesus' name (his will, character, and purpose) and for the glory of the Father. From an objective, Historical-Grammatical perspective, most prayers are answered through guidance and direction found in the Scriptures. Jehovah listens to those who humbly seek to serve Him in alignment with His will as revealed in the Bible. Therefore, our prayers are most effective when we are biblically minded, allowing the Holy Spirit-inspired Word of God to guide our thoughts and requests.

Conclusion: The Ultimate Objective—God's Glory

The goal of every prayer should be the glory of Jehovah, not the satisfaction of our desires. John 14:13 affirms this, saying, "Whatever you ask in my name, this I will do, that the Father may be glorified in the Son" (UASV). When our prayers are channeled toward this ultimate objective, unanswered prayers become less about personal disappointment and more about divine purpose. Therefore, as we strive to strengthen our prayer lives, may we focus less on the attainment of our requests and more on the magnification of Jehovah's glory.

SECTION 4 BIBLICAL ANSWERS TO THE DIFFICULT SUBJECTS

Dive deep into the Bible's challenging passages with "Biblical Answers to Difficult Subjects". Harnessing the Historical-Grammatical method, this guide illuminates contradictions, moral dilemmas, and profound truths, leading readers closer to God's intended message.

As with any literary work that has shaped civilizations and cultures for millennia, the Bible is not without its complexities and enigmatic passages. However, when approached with the correct hermeneutic method and an understanding of the historical, cultural, and linguistic backgrounds, these difficulties can be addressed coherently and faithfully.

Understanding the Nature of Difficulties

The term "difficulty" can denote various things when referring to the Bible. It might mean a perceived contradiction, a moral quandary, or a passage that seems historically implausible. But most often, it refers to passages that are challenging to understand or interpret within their context.

Historical Context: Much of the Bible was written in a time and culture vastly different from our own. Without understanding the historical setting in which a text was written, certain details or idioms might seem out of place or contradictory.

Linguistic Nuances: The Bible was written primarily in Hebrew, Aramaic, and Greek. When translating any text, especially ancient ones, some nuances and subtleties of the original languages might be lost or misinterpreted.

The Historical-Grammatical Method

An essential tool for the conservative Bible scholar is the **Historical-Grammatical method**. This method seeks to understand a text within its original historical context and its plain, ordinary grammatical sense. This method avoids speculative or allegorical interpretations and focuses on the author's original intent.

The Importance of Authorial Intent: Every author writes with a purpose. By understanding the context in which the author wrote, we can grasp the intended meaning more clearly.

Resisting the Urge for Allegory: Allegorical interpretations can sometimes diverge from the actual message of the text. Instead, by focusing on the plain meaning of the text, we remain anchored in the truth the Scripture intends to convey.

Addressing Alleged Contradictions

One of the primary difficulties that readers encounter is alleged contradictions within Scripture. Upon closer inspection, many of these "contradictions" can be reconciled by understanding the context or recognizing the different literary styles employed by the authors.

Parallel Accounts: The Bible often gives parallel accounts of the same event, especially in the Gospels. Differences in these accounts aren't contradictions but reflect the unique perspectives or emphasis of the individual authors.

Genre Considerations: Different books of the Bible fall into various genres – historical, poetic, prophetic, epistolary, and apocalyptic. Recognizing the genre can clarify passages that might otherwise seem contradictory or perplexing.

The Moral Quandaries

The Bible sometimes portrays actions or commands that might seem morally problematic from a modern perspective. However, it's crucial to differentiate between *descriptive* passages, which simply describe events, and *prescriptive* passages, which give commandments or moral teachings.

Historical Narratives: Just because an action is described in the Bible doesn't mean it is endorsed. Many accounts serve to show humanity's flawed nature and the consequences of sin.

Divine Commands: At times, God issued commands that might seem harsh. However, understanding the broader context, especially the covenantal relationship between God and His people, often sheds light on the reasons behind such commands.

Hell and the Nature of Punishment

There are multiple terms translated as "hell" in the Scriptures, such as *Hades*, *Sheol*, *Gehenna*, and *Tartarus*. However, rather than portraying hell as a place of eternal torment, these terms reflect the idea of eternal destruction or the grave.

Understanding "Eternal": The term "eternal" in the context of punishment often signifies a final and irreversible state rather than unending torment. The wicked are permanently removed from God's purpose for a righteous, inhabited earth.

The Nature of Humans: Souls, not Having Souls

Genesis 2:7 states that man became a "living soul" (nephesh). This crucial understanding underscores that humans don't *possess* souls; they *are* souls. This perspective aligns with the broader biblical teaching that life is a gift from God and that death is a cessation of existence, not an entrance into another form of conscious existence.

The Spirit and Guidance

While the Holy Spirit played active roles in the lives of certain individuals in the Scriptures, the notion of an "indwelling" of the Spirit in every believer is not a biblical teaching. Christians are guided by the Spirit-inspired Word of God, which serves as our compass and lamp in a darkened world.

God's Purpose for the Earth

God's purpose for the earth was for it to be inhabited, as stated in Isaiah 45:18. This underscores the hope that many Christians have for a restored paradise on earth, in line with the Lord's Prayer's plea for God's will to be done "on earth as it is in heaven."

Conclusion

While the Bible certainly has passages that challenge our understanding, approaching it with the right tools and a commitment to understanding its context can illuminate even the most perplexing verses. With reverence for the inspired Word of God and confidence in its coherence and truth, we can navigate its pages with both intellectual rigor and spiritual devotion. As with any profound and transformative text, the depth and richness of Scripture beckon us to study it earnestly, ever seeking the face of God and His purpose for humanity.

CHAPTER 12 How Can We Deal with Doubt and Unbelief?

Doubt and unbelief are challenges experienced by all Christians at some point. Understanding the difference between them is vital as each calls for a distinct approach. Intellectual, emotional, social, and spiritual doubts arise from different areas and can be addressed effectively through study, prayer, community, and introspection. Utilizing resources like Scripture guidance can transform these periods of doubt into times of growth and spiritual deepening.

In "How Can We Deal with Doubt and Unbelief?" we explore the nature, types, and sources of doubt and unbelief that Christians face. Understand how to approach these challenges through prayer, deep engagement with Scripture, and supportive community, transforming periods of doubt into opportunities for spiritual growth. Navigating the complexities of doubt and unbelief in Christian life is a common challenge. Learn how to differentiate between doubt and unbelief, identify their sources, and effectively address them through prayer, Scriptural guidance, and community support.

Doubt and unbelief are existential issues that every Christian, regardless of the depth of their faith, encounters at some point in their spiritual journey. It is crucial to understand that experiencing doubt is not tantamount to spiritual failure or an irrevocable fall from grace. Rather, how we approach and handle these doubts can either strengthen our faith or further estrange us from the foundation of our beliefs.

The Nature of Doubt and Unbelief

Doubt and **unbelief** are often used interchangeably, but they are not synonymous. Doubt can be best described as a state of uncertainty or hesitation in the face of questions or difficulties. It usually arises when we encounter scriptural complexities, ethical questions, or overwhelming personal experiences that challenge our long-held beliefs. On the other hand, unbelief is a more conscious, willful turning away from faith or a rejection of certain core Christian doctrines.

Understanding the difference between doubt and unbelief is vital because they necessitate different approaches for resolution. Doubt often needs information, reassurance, or a new perspective, while unbelief requires a more profound transformation of the heart and mind, which can often be more complex to address.

The Source of Doubts

Identifying the source of your doubt is the first step in addressing it effectively. Doubts can emanate from various areas:

1. **Intellectual Doubts**: These are doubts that stem from difficulties in understanding certain Scriptural passages or Christian doctrines. Examples include the problem of suffering, biblical chronology, or the complexities surrounding God's nature.
2. **Emotional Doubts**: These doubts often arise from personal suffering or the apparent incongruencies between the idea of a loving God and the reality of a broken world.
3. **Social Doubts**: Peer pressure, societal norms, or the opinions of people we respect can also induce doubt. The doubt in this case is usually linked to the fear of social isolation or ridicule.
4. **Spiritual Doubts**: Sometimes, doubt comes from within, especially when one goes through a period of spiritual dryness or perceives a lack of God's presence.

Tackling Intellectual Doubts

One of the most effective ways to address intellectual doubts is through rigorous study and the objective Historical-Grammatical method of interpreting Scriptures. It is essential to dig deep into the Word of God, employing exegetical tools and referring to conservative scholarship that aligns with your convictions. It's important to remember that "All Scripture is inspired by God and beneficial for teaching, for rebuke, for correction, for training in righteousness" (2 Timothy 3:16, UASV).

Addressing Emotional Doubts

Emotional doubts can be the most painful to experience, but they also offer an opportunity for profound spiritual growth. One must confront these doubts head-on by acknowledging their existence. Prayer is an invaluable resource in these times. Pour out your heart to God like David did in the Psalms.

We must also remember that God allows suffering, and our emotional doubts often arise from an incomplete or incorrect understanding of God's character and purposes. Delving into Scriptures that discuss suffering and God's sovereignty can provide a more rounded view of God's nature and how He operates in our lives.

Navigating Social Doubts

To navigate through social doubts, it's crucial to be rooted in a community that shares your conservative biblical values. While it may be challenging to voice doubts, a trusted community can provide scriptural insights, emotional support, and prayer.

Equally important is to understand that societal norms and opinions are ever-changing, but "the word of our God endures forever" (Isaiah 40:8, UASV). Upholding scriptural truths may sometimes make you counter-cultural, but that is often the cost of genuine faith.

Combatting Spiritual Doubts

For spiritual doubts, one needs to engage in deep self-examination. Are there unrepented sins or ungodly motives clouding your relationship with God? If so, repentance and realignment with God's will are essential.

Doubt as a Catalyst for Growth

When approached constructively, doubt can serve as a catalyst for deeper understanding and spiritual growth. It can lead you to intense study, prayer, and a renewed commitment to God. Ultimately, it is not the presence of doubt but how we deal with it that determines its impact on our spiritual lives.

The Role of Prayer and Scriptural Guidance

Prayer, coupled with a deep engagement with Scripture, is crucial in overcoming doubt and unbelief. Our prayers are most effective when we are biblically minded because our thinking is naturally guided by God, that is, His Word, the Bible. While God has a long-range view of matters and may not always grant our requests, He does provide the wisdom and guidance we need to navigate through our periods of doubt and unbelief.

Conclusion

Doubt and unbelief are not uncommon experiences in the Christian journey. However, how we deal with them is crucial. Utilizing resources like prayer, conservative scholarship, and community can turn periods of doubt into seasons of growth. But most importantly, the role of Scripture cannot be overemphasized. For "the word of God is living and active and sharper than any two-edged sword" (Hebrews 4:12, UASV), and it is the primary means by which we can gain the wisdom to navigate the complexities of doubt and unbelief.

CHAPTER 13 Our Struggle Against Dark Spiritual Forces

The chapter discusses the Christian concept of spiritual warfare. It emphasizes the reality of Satan and dark spiritual forces, asserting that they actively oppose God's plan and attempt to lead people away from Him. The article outlines Satan's tactics—deception, temptation, and accusation—and articulates the spiritual armory available to believers, including truth, righteousness, faith, and Scripture. It reaffirms the importance of community and vigilance in combating these forces and highlights the believer's ultimate reliance on God.

The chapter offers an understanding of the spiritual warfare Christians are engaged in. Learn about Satan's tactics, the hierarchy of dark spiritual forces, and how to equip yourself with the armor of God. Discover the role of vigilance and community in fortifying your spiritual life against these nefarious forces.

The battle against Satan and dark spiritual forces is an essential aspect of the Christian life that requires both discernment and equipping. Apostle Paul states in Ephesians 6:12, "For our struggle is not against flesh and blood, but against the rulers, against the authorities, against the cosmic powers of this darkness, against evil, spiritual forces in the heavens" (UASV). This chapter aims to unveil the reality, nature, and strategies of these dark forces and how a believer can stand strong in the midst of this spiritual warfare.

Understanding the Nature of the Battle

Before we delve into the strategies for warfare, it is crucial to understand the nature of the battle we are engaged in. This is not a physical battle but a spiritual one, often waged in the mind and the heart. This is a battle against rebellious spiritual entities whose primary goal is to oppose God's plan and lead people away from Him. These entities operate under the authority of Satan, the chief adversary of God and humanity.

The Reality of Satan

Satan is not a fictional character or a metaphorical representation of evil; he is a real, personal being. Scriptures describe him as a fallen angel who rebelled against God and was consequently cast down from heaven (Isaiah 14:12-15; Ezekiel 28:12-17). He is also identified as "the god of this age" who blinds the minds of unbelievers (2 Corinthians 4:4, UASV). His work primarily involves sowing discord, promoting false teachings, and leading people into sin.

The Hierarchy of Dark Spiritual Forces

The term "dark spiritual forces" refers to a range of evil spiritual entities that operate under Satan's command. Paul, in Ephesians 6:12, identifies these as rulers, authorities, and cosmic powers. While the Bible doesn't provide a detailed taxonomy, it's clear that there is an organized structure of dark forces working against God's kingdom.

Satan's Modus Operandi

Understanding how Satan operates is crucial for effective spiritual warfare. Among his primary tactics are:

1. **Deception**: Satan is referred to as the "father of lies" (John 8:44, UASV). He deceives through false doctrines, counterfeit religions, and twisted interpretations of Scriptures.

2. **Temptation**: He tempts believers to commit sins that separate them from God's will, exploiting their weaknesses and desires.

3. **Accusation**: Satan is also called "the accuser of our brothers" (Revelation 12:10, UASV). He uses guilt and shame to keep believers in a state of spiritual paralysis.

The Believer's Armory

In Ephesians 6:10-18, Paul outlines the spiritual armor that believers must put on to stand against the devil's schemes. These include:

1. **The Belt of Truth**: Being grounded in the truth of God's word protects us against Satan's deceptions.

2. **The Breastplate of Righteousness**: Living a life of moral integrity safeguards us from the temptations that Satan places in our path.

3. **The Shield of Faith**: Our faith in God and His promises enable us to quench all the fiery darts of the evil one.

4. **The Sword of the Spirit**: This refers to the word of God, which is our primary offensive weapon against the enemy.

Spiritual Vigilance

Believers are called to be vigilant because "your adversary, the devil, prowls around like a roaring lion, seeking someone to devour" (1 Peter 5:8, UASV). This involves being watchful in prayer, rooted in Scriptures, and mindful of the schemes of the devil.

Community as a Stronghold

The Christian community serves as a significant resource in the fight against dark spiritual forces. James advises believers to "confess your sins to one another and pray for one another, that you may be healed" (James 5:16, UASV). A community founded on prayer and the study of Scriptures creates an environment where believers can stand strong against the enemy's attacks.

Conclusion

The struggle against dark spiritual forces is a reality that every believer must come to terms with. Understanding the enemy, being aware of his tactics, and putting on the full armor of God are prerequisites for standing strong in this spiritual battle. However, we do not fight alone. We have the community of believers and, most importantly, the Word of God to guide and protect us. As we remain vigilant and rooted in Scripture, we can face these dark forces with the assurance that "He who is in you is greater than he who is in the world" (1 John 4:4, UASV).

APPENDIX A How Can We Reconcile Our Faith with the Realities of the World Around Us?

This chapter presents strategies to reconcile faith with issues such as intellectual doubt, ethical complications, and supposed conflict between science and faith. It discusses Christian apologetics, treating faith as complementary to science, using biblical ethical framework for social challenges, comprehending the theology of suffering and maintaining faith amid cultural engagement. The aim is to strengthen and defend faith amid modern complexities, grounding it in Scriptural understanding.

Navigating faith in today's world is complex but not impossible. The appendix "How Can We Reconcile Our Faith with the Realities of the World Around Us?" offers comprehensive strategies and biblical principles to strengthen and defend your faith amid intellectual doubt, ethical dilemmas, and the so-called conflict between science and faith. Become equipped to make your faith unshakable.

For many, reconciling faith with the realities of the world around us is a challenging endeavor. The paradoxes seem insurmountable—how can a loving God allow suffering? Why does faith seem to clash with scientific inquiry? How should a Christian navigate through social issues that appear to challenge biblical norms? This appendix aims to address these issues head-on and provide an analytical framework within which faith not only survives but thrives amid the complexities of modern life.

The Challenge of Intellectual Doubt

Intellectual doubt is often the first stumbling block for believers. Questions about the accuracy of Scriptures, the existence of God, or the relevance of the Christian worldview in a pluralistic society are bound to surface. Intellectual doubt, however, should not be equated with a lack of faith. Rather, it can serve as a catalyst for a deeper exploration of one's beliefs.

The Role of Apologetics

Christian apologetics, which involves the defense of the faith against objections, plays a crucial role in reconciling faith and reason. A robust apologetic method involves understanding arguments for the existence of God, the historicity of Christ's resurrection, and the reliability of Scriptures, among others. Far from discouraging questions, this field invites scrutiny and appeals to evidence and reason.

Science and Faith: An Apparent Conflict

One of the most debated issues is the supposed conflict between science and faith. It's crucial to recognize that both science and faith answer different kinds of questions—science deals with the "how," while faith addresses the "why."

Faith as Complementary to Science

The believer should understand that faith complements science rather than contradicts it. While science can explain the mechanisms of evolution, for instance, it cannot answer questions about the purpose of life. Thus, one can be a rigorous scientist and a devout Christian, understanding that each field has its own domain of inquiry.

Social and Ethical Challenges

The modern era has presented new ethical and social challenges, including issues like abortion, gender identity, and social justice. Navigating these waters can be particularly tricky for Christians, who must reconcile their faith with the ever-evolving societal norms that are contrary to God's Word.

Biblical Ethical Framework

The Bible provides an ethical framework that can guide the Christian's engagement with these issues. This framework doesn't change with societal norms but stands as a fixed point of reference. While the application may require nuanced approaches, the ethical principles themselves are immutable.

The Problem of Suffering

One of the most emotionally charged issues is the problem of suffering. How can an all-powerful, all-loving God allow suffering to exist?

A Theology of Suffering

Scripture teaches that God allows suffering for various reasons, none of which imply a lack of divine love or power. Some suffering is the result of human sin, while other forms serve to build character, deepen faith, or fulfill God's greater plan. While this doesn't remove the emotional weight of suffering, it provides a framework within which suffering can be understood and even redeemed.

Faith and Culture: Being in the World but Not of It

Christians are called to be salt and light in the world (Matthew 5:13-16), but this requires a delicate balance. How can one be "in the world" but not "of the world" (John 17:14-16)?

Faith as Cultural Engagement

Engagement with culture requires discernment. The Christian should neither withdraw from the world nor conform to it but should act as an agent of transformation. This involves critically interacting with cultural products, advocating for biblical values, and serving as a witness to Christ in all spheres of life.

Conclusion

Reconciling faith with the complexities of modern life is undoubtedly a challenge. However, it's a challenge that invites deeper exploration, nuanced understanding, and robust defense of the Christian worldview. Intellectual doubt, social issues, the problem of suffering, and even apparent conflicts with science can be understood better through the lens of a mature faith grounded in Scriptures. It is not a blind leap into the abyss but a reasoned trust in the God who is the same "yesterday and today and forever" (Hebrews 13:8, UASV). With such an anchor, the believer is well-equipped to navigate the tumultuous waters of contemporary life, making their faith truly unshakable.

APPENDIX B Why Is Life So Unfair?

The appendix discusses the theological and philosophical issues around life's unfairness, focusing on the Christian perspective. It emphasizes the role of human sin and the free will God grants us as sources of suffering and injustice. The discussion revolves around biblical teachings and asserts that God will eventually rectify all injustices. It provocatively asserts that Christians should live justly and embrace the world's unfairness with faith, hope, and courage.

Why Is Life So Unfair?

Introduction: The Perennial Question of Inequity

The question of why life is so unfair is one that has echoed through human history. It transcends cultures, religions, and personal philosophies, affecting us all at one point or another. When we observe the suffering of innocent people, the prosperity of the wicked, and the apparent randomness of good and bad circumstances, the question becomes not just intellectual but deeply emotional. *How can we reconcile a belief in a just and loving God with the glaring inequities we see in the world?*

The Problem of Evil and Suffering

Before we delve into the question of life's unfairness, it is imperative to acknowledge the broader theological and philosophical issue known as the problem of evil and suffering. In essence, if God is all-good, all-powerful, and all-knowing, why is there evil and suffering in the world?

Human Sin and Its Consequences

First and foremost, it's important to note that the Bible teaches that much of the suffering and injustice in the world is a direct or indirect result of human sin. From the disobedience of Adam and Eve in the Garden of Eden to the individual and collective sins that humans commit daily, sin has a corrupting effect on the world (Romans 5:12; 8:22). This corruption manifests in various forms, including moral evils like greed and violence, and natural evils such as disease and disasters.

God's Sovereignty and Human Freedom

The Bible also upholds the concept of human freedom and moral agency. While God is sovereign, He allows humans to exercise free will, even when their choices lead to injustice and suffering. This freedom is essential for love and moral virtue to be possible, but it also means that inequity and evil are the price we pay for freedom (Deuteronomy 30:19; Joshua 24:15).

Biblical Perspectives on Life's Unfairness

The Book of Job: Suffering and Divine Wisdom

The Book of Job tackles the issue of unjust suffering head-on. Job, a righteous man, faces extreme suffering not as a result of his sins but due to circumstances that are beyond his control and understanding. The takeaway from Job is not a neat answer to why life is unfair but an invitation to trust in God's wisdom and sovereignty even when we don't understand His ways (Job 42:1-6).

The Psalms: Lament and Trust

The Psalms are replete with laments about injustice, suffering, and the prosperity of the wicked (e.g., Psalm 73; 37). Yet they also consistently point to the justice of God and the ultimate vindication of the righteous. The lesson here is that it's okay to bring our questions and complaints to God, but we should do so in a posture of trust and reverence.

The Teachings of Jesus and the Apostles

Jesus Himself was no stranger to suffering and injustice, having been crucified despite His innocence. His teachings and those of His apostles affirm the reality of suffering and injustice in this world while also promising that God will set things right in the end (Matthew 5:10-12; Romans 8:18; 2 Corinthians 4:17).

The Christian Hope: God Will Set Things Right

Despite the brokenness of the world, the Christian faith offers a robust hope: the promise that God will eventually set things right. This is evident in numerous biblical passages that speak of the coming judgment, the resurrection of the dead, and the creation of a new heavens and a new earth where justice will reign (2 Peter 3:13; Revelation 21:1-4).

The Cosmic Scope of Redemption

It's worth emphasizing that the Christian hope is not merely individual but cosmic in scope. The redemption purchased by Jesus on the cross is not just for human souls but for the entire created order (Romans 8:19-23). This means that God's ultimate answer to life's unfairness is not just to "balance the scales" for individuals but to restore righteousness and justice to the whole universe.

Practical Implications: Living Justly in an Unjust World

Understanding the theological and eschatological aspects of life's unfairness should lead to practical applications. *Christians are called to be agents of justice and righteousness in the world.* This means actively combating injustice, helping those who suffer, and advocating for fairness and equity in society (Micah 6:8; James 1:27).

Conclusion: Faith Amidst the Unfairness

While the question of why life is so unfair may never be fully answered in this life, the Christian faith provides a framework for navigating this complex issue. Grounded in the understanding of human sin, the respect for human freedom, and the trust in divine wisdom, believers can face life's inequities not with cynicism but with a robust hope. God is just, and He will set things right, both in individual lives and in the cosmos. This hope, coupled with a commitment to live justly, enables Christians to face the unfairness of life with faith and courage.

APPENDIX C How Can We Live a Life That Is Pleasing to God?

Christian living requires pleasing God through faith, obedience, repentance, worship, service to others, financial stewardship, and resilience during trials. It isn't about rule-following but about living out a relationship with God. These actions are seen as expressions of love and commitment, not ways to earn God's favor. The ultimate goal is eternal rewards, emphasizing a perspective that looks beyond the current world of wicked mankind.

The Paramount Importance of Pleasing God

To be a Christian is not merely a matter of professing faith but living it out in everyday life. Our ultimate objective should be to please God in all our endeavors. It isn't a matter of earning our salvation, which is by grace through faith (Ephesians 2:8-9). Rather, it is the natural response to a loving relationship with our Creator. This quest for pleasing God is not a trivial pursuit; it is the very essence of a Christian's earthly existence.

The Role of Faith in Pleasing God

The foundation for any attempt to please God must be faith. As Hebrews 11:6 reminds us, "without faith, it is impossible to please him, for whoever would draw near to God must believe that he exists and that he rewards those who seek him." Faith is not merely intellectual assent but a complete trust in God that leads to obedience.

Obedience and God's Commandments

It is a misunderstanding to think that we can please God by our efforts alone or through a checklist of moral deeds. In reality, obedience to God's commandments is a manifestation of our faith and love for Him. As 1 John 5:3 states, "For this is the love of God, that we keep his commandments. And his commandments are not burdensome."

The Necessity of Repentance and Transformation

A Christian cannot continue to live in sin and expect to please God. Repentance is not just a one-time act but a continuous process. This requires not just turning away from sin but also a transformation of one's life by the renewing of the mind (Romans 12:2). God's Spirit-inspired Word helps in this transformation.

Living a Life of Prayer and Worship

A life pleasing to God is one steeped in prayer and worship. It is through these spiritual disciplines that we develop a deep and intimate relationship with God. However, it's crucial to remember that we don't conjure God's presence or favor through these activities. They are means of grace that align our will with God's will.

Being a Witness and Serving Others

Living a life that pleases God isn't solely about our individual relationship with Him; it also involves how we relate to others. Sharing the gospel and serving others are not just good deeds but are acts of obedience to God's commandments (Matthew 28:19-20). By doing so, we reflect the character of Christ to a broken world.

Financial Stewardship and Generosity

The way we manage our finances also reveals our heart's allegiance. The Bible teaches the importance of giving a portion of our income to God's work and serving those in need. This isn't a means to earn favor but an act of worship and a practical way to acknowledge that everything we have comes from God (1 Timothy 6:17-19).

Navigating Trials and Suffering

Life's inevitable difficulties are not arbitrary events but are either allowed or designed by God for our spiritual refinement. In facing these trials, a continued trust in God and adherence to His ways are the hallmarks of a life pleasing to Him (James 1:2-4).

The Eternal Perspective: Our Ultimate Reward

Our pursuit to live a life pleasing to God is not just for temporal benefits. The ultimate reward awaits us in eternity, where we will be in the direct presence of God, receiving the words, "Well done, good and faithful servant" (Matthew 25:21). Therefore, the life we lead here should be lived in the light of eternity.

Conclusion

Living a life that pleases God is a multi-faceted endeavor that requires faith, obedience, repentance, a life of worship, service to others, financial stewardship, and resilience during trials. It is not a quest for the faint of heart but one that offers eternal rewards. The quest for pleasing God does not stem from a legalistic observance of rules but from a heart transformed by a relationship with God through His Son, Jesus Christ. The Holy Spirit-inspired Word serves as our primary guide in this lifelong journey. We are not alone in this endeavor; we have the eternal promises of God and the fellowship of the body of Christ to support us. Therefore, let us strive every day, with every fiber of our being, to live a life that is pleasing to God.

APPENDIX D How Can We Find Out What God Requires of Us?

Understanding what God requires of us involves more than just superficial Bible reading. Understanding what God requires of us requires serious attention, study, and internalizing spiritual principles. It involves studying the Scriptures, learning from spiritually mature individuals, and applying these principles in our lives. This comprehension of God's expectations helps align our lives with His will. Sources of understanding include the Bible, external resources, prayer, Christian community, trials, and spiritual mentorship. However, understanding God's requirements is a lifelong commitment and not an overnight task.

Understanding what God requires of us is a subject that requires serious attention and dedicated study. It involves delving into the Scriptures, being receptive to guidance from spiritually mature individuals, and deeply internalizing spiritual principles. The clarity with which we understand God's expectations correlates with how well we can align our lives with His will.

The Primacy of Scripture

The most straightforward way to discover what God requires of us is through the study of His inspired Word, the Bible. The Bible itself asserts its own sufficiency for teaching, reproof, correction, and training in righteousness (2 Timothy 3:16-17). In the Old Testament, Jehovah made His expectations clear through the Law and the Prophets. In the New Testament, we find the teachings of Jesus and the apostles providing a fuller understanding of God's requirements.

Personal Study and Mediation

Direct engagement with the Bible allows one to connect with the very thoughts of God. Study should be approached using the historical-grammatical method, treating the text with the respect it deserves as a literary document inspired by God. This method offers insights into the historical context, literary forms, and original languages of the Scriptures.

External Sources

While the Bible should always be the primary source for understanding God's requirements, trusted commentaries, Bible dictionaries, and lexicons can provide additional insights. The key is to ensure that these secondary sources don't overshadow the Biblical text but assist in revealing its intended message.

The Role of Prayer

Prayer isn't merely a ritual but an essential part of our relationship with God. James 1:5 tells us that if we lack wisdom, we should ask God. However, it's worth noting that while God listens to our prayers, He does not indwell us. The answer to our prayers often comes through the guidance of the Spirit-inspired Word of God.

Accountability to the Christian Community

The early Christian congregations placed great emphasis on the collective understanding of Scripture (Acts 17:11). Being a part of a community allows for collective wisdom and differing perspectives that can enhance one's understanding of what God requires.

Spiritual Mentorship

Mature Christians often provide much-needed guidance in navigating complex Biblical truths. This mentorship isn't meant to replace personal study but to complement it.

Trial and Error

Our lives are often the best testing ground for what we glean from the Scriptures. Sometimes, what God requires of us becomes clearest when we're in the midst of challenges. We must remember that "we do not have a soul, we are souls," and our entire being is engaged in this journey of conforming to God's will. Even when we falter, the Scriptures provide us with the means for correction and setting our path straight once more.

The Role of Christian Ethics

The ethical principles laid out in the Scriptures give us practical guidelines for daily living. From the Ten Commandments to the Sermon on the Mount, we find a moral framework that's meant to be applied consistently and diligently.

Conclusions

Understanding what God requires of us is not an overnight task. It requires diligent study of the Scriptures, prayer, engagement with the Christian community, and practical application in our daily lives. There's no shortcut to this; it's a lifelong commitment. However, the rewards for taking this commitment seriously are eternal, as our lives slowly but surely align with the divine will. Therefore, let us endeavor to understand God's requirements not merely as rules to be followed but as the pathway to a fulfilling, meaningful relationship with our Creator.

Edward D. Andrews

APPENDIX E In What Ways Must God's Servants Be Clean?

The appendix discusses the importance of cleanliness as a multifaceted concept, encompassing physical hygiene, moral integrity, and spiritual purity for believers. It emphasizes that cleanliness goes beyond physical hygiene to include upholding ethical standards, sexual purity, adhering to sound doctrine, maintaining a robust prayer life, and cultivating healthy relationships. The ultimate aim is achieving holiness and fulfilling God's divine purpose.

The Theological Foundation of Cleanliness

The Scriptures repeatedly emphasize the significance of cleanliness in the lives of God's servants. The Apostle Paul makes it clear in 2 Corinthians 7:1 that believers are to "cleanse ourselves from every defilement of body and spirit, bringing holiness to completion in the fear of God." This statement encapsulates the essence of cleanliness as a multifaceted concept, encompassing not only physical cleanliness but also moral and spiritual purity.

Physical Cleanliness

Bodily Hygiene

Physical cleanliness, although the most basic form, cannot be overlooked. Being well-groomed and maintaining bodily hygiene are essential for representing God properly to others. The Temple in Jerusalem, with its stringent purification rituals, serves as a model for the meticulous care God expects in our personal hygiene.

Environmental Cleanliness

The Scriptures also discuss environmental cleanliness. For example, the law given to Israel specified how waste should be properly disposed of outside the camp. In the present day, this extends to responsible stewardship of the Earth, which God created for mankind's benefit.

Moral Cleanliness

Ethical Integrity

Being morally clean involves upholding the ethical standards presented in the Scriptures. This means standing firm against lying, cheating, stealing, and other forms of deception or corruption. Moral cleanliness is about embodying the principles that God has established for just and ethical living. James 1:27 even equates pure and undefiled religion with keeping oneself unstained from the world.

Sexual Purity

Sexual purity is another facet of moral cleanliness. The Bible is clear that sexual relations are to be enjoyed exclusively within the bounds of a marriage between a man and a woman. Sexual immorality in any form—adultery, fornication, or even lustful thoughts—is in direct violation of God's design and commandments.

Spiritual Cleanliness

Right Doctrine

Spiritual cleanliness starts with adhering to sound doctrine. False teachings are likened to gangrene in the New Testament, and thus, a clear understanding of biblical truth is essential for maintaining spiritual purity.

Communion with God

Maintaining a robust prayer life and continuous Bible study contributes to spiritual cleanliness. Prayer allows for the confession of sin and for seeking guidance from God, while the study of Scripture helps one remain rooted in God's commandments.

Relationships

Being spiritually clean also affects one's relationships. This includes fellowship within the body of Christ and extends to how one interacts with non-believers. Unhealthy relationships can taint one's spiritual walk, so it's essential to maintain relationships that honor God.

The Ultimate Objective: Holiness

The ultimate objective of being clean in these various aspects is holiness—being set apart for God's service. Being clean isn't an end in itself but a means to fulfill God's purpose for our lives. Peter encapsulates this when he writes, "But as He who called you is holy, you also be holy in all your conduct" (1 Peter 1:15).

Conclusion

Cleanliness, in the eyes of God, is a comprehensive term involving physical hygiene, moral integrity, and spiritual purity. Failing to uphold standards in any one area can compromise our effectiveness as God's servants. Therefore, it is essential to be vigilant and proactive in maintaining cleanliness, all with the aim of glorifying God and fulfilling His divine purpose for our lives.

APPENDIX F What Are the Practices That God Hates?

This exploration discusses practices that God disapproves of, as stated in the Bible, aiming to inspire understanding and change. God hates falsehood, injustice, pride, shedding innocent blood, idolatry, sexual immorality, and divisiveness among believers. Appreciating these prohibitions offers insight into God's nature, helping believers align themselves with His will to establish a stronger connection with Him.

Understanding what God hates is indispensable to living a life that is aligned with His will and directives. The Bible clearly delineates actions, attitudes, and practices that are abominable to God. This detailed exploration aims to bring these to light, not merely as prohibitions but as insights into the nature and character of God. In the Bible, we find that God hates falsehood, injustice, pride, and other sinful behaviors. *The purpose is not to instill fear, but to promote understanding and inspire change.*

Falsehood and Deception

God hates falsehood and deception. *Proverbs 12:22* asserts, "Lying lips are detestable to Jehovah, but those who deal faithfully are His delight." Falsehood not only disrupts the social fabric but also stands in direct contradiction to the nature of God, who is Truth. Being truthful in all dealings, whether big or small, aligns us more closely with the divine will.

Injustice and Unfairness

Injustice is another area that God strongly disapproves of. Amos 5:15 instructs, "Hate evil, and love good, and establish justice in the gate." The prophet Micah summarizes God's requirements as doing justice, loving kindness, and walking humbly with God (Micah 6:8). *Any form of injustice, whether social, economic, or personal, is repugnant to God.*

Pride and Arrogance

Proverbs 8:13 says, "The fear of Jehovah is to hate evil; I hate pride and arrogance, evil behavior, and a perverse mouth." God despises pride and arrogance because they set human beings in opposition to Him. Humility is not just a social grace but a requirement for a right relationship with God.

Shedding of Innocent Blood

The act of taking innocent lives is detestable to God. Numerous Scriptures bear witness to this fact. *For instance, Proverbs 6:16–17* mentions "hands that shed innocent blood" among the things that God hates. Respect for life is not a mere ethical norm but a reflection of the God who gives life.

Idolatry

The Bible is explicit that God hates idolatry. *Deuteronomy 12:31* makes it clear that God finds the practices of idol-worshipers abominable. Idolatry is a violation of the first commandment and undermines the exclusive worship due to God.

Sexual Immorality

Sexual immorality is strongly condemned in the Bible. From the illicit relations depicted in *1 Corinthians 6:18–20* to the strong language in Hebrews 13:4, it's clear that sexual purity is critical to a life pleasing to God. He designed sexuality to be enjoyed within the bounds of a committed marital relationship, and any deviation from this is against His divine plan.

Divisiveness and Contentions

God hates divisions and contentions among believers. *The Apostle Paul warns against divisions in 1 Corinthians 1:10*, urging believers to be united in thought and judgment. God desires His Church to reflect His unity and love, making divisiveness particularly displeasing to Him.

Conclusion

Understanding what God hates is integral for believers who aim to live lives that are pleasing to Him. Such understanding not only helps us avoid certain behaviors but also gives us a richer comprehension of God's nature. As we align ourselves with God's likes and dislikes, we draw closer to Him and fulfill the purpose for which we were created. *Scripture offers us the clearest lens through which we can understand these important matters*, always being the ultimate authority on what practices are abominable to God.

APPENDIX G What Are the Markers of a True Christian?

The appendix outlines the markers of a true Christian in a world laden with religious pluralism and doctrinal ambiguity. These markers, founded on faith, love, and hope, include faith deeply rooted in scripture, repentance and redemption through Jesus Christ, a personal relationship with Jesus, love as a defining characteristic, Holy Spirit-inspired moral and ethical conduct, involvement in a local church, evangelism, discipleship, and the hope of resurrection. These non-negotiable identifiers shape a true Christian's beliefs, actions, and lifestyle.

Introduction: The Imperative of Christian Identity

In the age of religious pluralism and doctrinal ambiguity, one question arises with paramount importance: What makes a true Christian? **Markers of a True Christian** delineate not only the set of beliefs but also the lifestyle and moral choices that align with God's Word. With the increasing adoption of a generic form of Christianity that often compromises on foundational truths, understanding these markers becomes a spiritual imperative.

Faith Rooted in Scripture

The true cornerstone of Christian identity is faith that is entirely rooted in Scripture. For those who hold the Bible as divinely inspired, it becomes the ultimate guide for faith and practice. Paul aptly encapsulates this by stating, "All Scripture is breathed out by God and profitable for teaching, for reproof, for correction, and for training in righteousness" (2 Timothy 3:16, UASV). A Christian whose beliefs are deeply rooted in the Bible will exhibit a lifestyle that aligns with Scriptural principles.

Repentance and Redemption

Fundamental to Christian identity is the concept of repentance and redemption through Jesus Christ. Acts 3:19 (UASV) says, "Repent therefore, and turn back, that your sins may be blotted out." This process of turning away from sin towards righteousness is enabled by the redemptive work of Jesus Christ on the cross.

Personal Relationship with Jesus Christ

Having a personal relationship with Jesus Christ is another crucial marker. This goes beyond a superficial acknowledgment of Christ and extends into an intimate, ongoing relationship with Him. This involves daily communion through prayer, obedience to His teachings, and following His example. "I am the vine; you are the branches. Whoever abides in me and I in him, he it is that bears much fruit, for apart from me you can do nothing" (John 15:5, UASV).

Love: The Defining Characteristic

Jesus Himself highlights love as the defining characteristic of His followers. In the Gospel of John, He states, "By this all people will know that you are my disciples, if you have love for one another" (John 13:35, UASV). Authentic Christian love extends not only to fellow believers but also to enemies, thereby reflecting the radical love of God.

Holy Spirit-Inspired Moral and Ethical Conduct

While the Holy Spirit does not indwell in us, we are guided by the Spirit-inspired Word of God. This guidance results in moral and ethical conduct that aligns with the fruit of the Spirit: love, joy, peace, patience, kindness, goodness, faithfulness, gentleness, and self-control (Galatians 5:22-23). These fruits manifest themselves in all aspects of life, pointing to the authenticity of one's faith.

Involvement in a Local Church Body

Consistent involvement in a local church body provides evidence of a believer's commitment to spiritual growth and Christian fellowship. Hebrews 10:25 (UASV) admonishes us not to forsake the assembly of believers, highlighting the importance of communal worship and mutual edification.

Evangelism and Discipleship

The Great Commission (Matthew 28:19-20) makes it clear that evangelism and discipleship are not optional activities but commandments for all true Christians. Being a witness to the Gospel and making disciples are activities that stem from an unshakeable belief in the salvific power of Jesus Christ.

The Hope of Resurrection

Lastly, the hope of resurrection and eternal life is a marker that distinguishes true Christians. This hope is not wishful thinking but a confident assurance based on the resurrection of Jesus Christ. It influences the believer's worldview, ethical decisions, and overall lifestyle, fortifying them against the existential doubts that plague secular minds.

Conclusion: The Non-Negotiables of Christian Identity

As we have seen, the markers of a true Christian encompass a complex but coherent identity founded on faith, love, and hope. These markers are non-negotiables, and any form of Christianity that lacks or compromises them should be subject to critical examination. In a world teeming with spiritual confusion, these markers act as the litmus test for true Christian faith. Therefore, each believer must continuously examine himself or herself in light of these markers, ever striving to be true followers of Jesus Christ.

Edward D. Andrews

APPENDIX H How Can We Help Others to Do God's Will?

The appendix stresses the collective responsibility of Christians in promoting spiritual growth and God's will through various means. These include discipleship, effective gospel communication, providing spiritual support, maintaining sound doctrine, nurturing local church communities, and actively participating in evangelism and outreach activities. This process, as outlined, not only helps in personal spiritual development but also assists others in knowing and living God's will.

Introduction: The Integral Role of Christians in Spiritual Nourishment

Living a life in harmony with God's will is not a solitary endeavor. The Scriptures emphasize the importance of communal relationships in achieving this spiritual aim. As part of the body of Christ, each individual has the responsibility not only to seek God's will for themselves but also to assist others in this quest. This appendix explores the ways in which we can help others to do God's will, in accordance with sound biblical principles.

Understanding the Importance of Discipleship

Discipleship is the cornerstone of spiritual growth. It's not enough to accept Christ and then live in isolation. We are instructed to "go therefore and make disciples" (Matthew 28:19, UASV). This involves helping others to know, understand, and apply the teachings of Scripture. Discipleship is an intentional act of guiding another in his or her walk with God, equipping them to fulfill His will in all aspects of life.

The Role of Effective Communication

The ability to effectively communicate the truth of the Gospel is critical. **Peter encourages us to be "always ready to give a defense to everyone who asks you a reason for the hope that is in you, with meekness and fear"** (1 Peter 3:15, UASV). Being able to articulate your faith clearly and coherently is essential for helping others to do God's will. This not only includes overt preaching but also living in such a way that your life becomes a testament to the Gospel message.

Providing Spiritual Support and Encouragement

It's not uncommon for individuals to struggle with spiritual doubt, disobedience, or disinterest. As fellow believers, it's our duty to offer spiritual support and encouragement. **The Apostle Paul reminds us to "bear one another's burdens, and so fulfill the law of Christ" (Galatians 6:2, UASV).** By being there for others in their times of spiritual weakness, we enable them to better align their lives with God's will.

Educating Through Sound Doctrine

One cannot underestimate the importance of sound doctrine in helping others do God's will. As Paul told Timothy, "All Scripture is inspired by God and profitable for teaching, for reproof, for correction, for training in righteousness" (2 Timothy 3:16, UASV). **Sound doctrine equips the believer with the principles and guidance they need to live in accord with God's will.** A flawed understanding can lead to actions that are misaligned with God's will, thereby causing spiritual confusion and stagnation.

Nurturing Local Church Communities

The local church is the bedrock of spiritual nourishment and growth. Paul's letters to various churches underline the importance of a unified and spiritually mature church body. **The church is instrumental in fostering an environment where believers can be equipped to do God's will.** This involves pastoral care, corporate worship, and participation in the sacraments, all of which edify the believer and prepare him or her to do God's will more fully.

Evangelism and Outreach

Lastly, we must remember that helping others to do God's will also includes those who have not yet come to faith. Jesus Himself was a friend to sinners and outcasts, always aiming to bring them into the fold of God's will. **Evangelism is not merely about 'winning souls,' but about making disciples who will do God's will.** Outreach programs, missionary activities, and personal evangelism are all avenues through which we can help others to know and do God's will.

Conclusion: The Collective Duty to Promote God's Will

As followers of Christ, we have an obligation not only to seek God's will for our lives but to help others do the same. **This involves a multifaceted approach that includes discipleship, effective communication, spiritual support, sound doctrine, a nurturing church community, and active evangelism.** By earnestly committing ourselves to these tasks, we fulfill the mandate given to us by Christ and play our part in bringing about the kingdom of God.

With these guiding principles, we can help others draw closer to God, achieve spiritual growth, and fulfill their God-given purpose. It's a lifelong endeavor, but one that comes with eternal rewards.

BIBLIOGRAPH

Akin, Daniel L. *The New American Commentary: 1, 2, 3 John.* Nashville, TN: Broadman & Holman , 2001.

Alden, Robert L. *Job, The New American Commentary, vol. 11* . Nashville: Broadman & Holman Publishers, 2001.

Anders, Max. *Holman New Testament Commentary: vol. 8, Galatians, Ephesians, Philippians, Colossians.* Nashville, TN: Broadman & Holman Publishers, 1999.

—. *Holman Old Testament Commentary - Proverbs* . Nashville: B&H Publishing, 2005.

Anders, Max, and Doug McIntosh. *Holman Old Testament Commentary - Deuteronomy.* Nashville: B&H Publishing, 2009.

Anders, Max, and Steven Lawson. *Holman Old Testament Commentary - Psalms: 11.* Grand Rapids: B&H Publishing, 2004.

Anders, Max, and Trent Butler. *Holman Old Testament Commentary: Isaiah.* Nashiville, TN: B&H Publishing, 2002.

Andrews, Stephen J, and Robert D Bergen. *Holman Old Testament Commentary: 1-2 Samuel.* Nashville: Broadman & Holman, 2009.

Balz, Horst, and Gerhard Schneider. *Exegetical Dictionary of the New Testament.* Edinburgh: T & T Clark Ltd, 1978.

Barker, Kenneth L., and Waylon Bailey. *The New American Commentary: vol. 20, Micah, Nahum, Habakkuk, Zephaniah.* Nashville, TN: Broadman & Holman Publishers, 2001.

Barry, John D., and Lazarus Wentz. *The Lexham Bible Dictionary.* Bellingham, WA: Logos Bible Software, 2012.

Benner, David G., and Peter C Hill. *Baker Encyclopedia of Psychology and Counseling (Second Edition).* Grand Rapids: Baker Books, 1985, 1999.

Bercot, David W. *A Dictionary of Early Christian Beliefs.* Peabody: Hendrickson, 1998.

Bergen, Robert D. *The New American Commentary: 1-2 Samuel.* Nashville: Broadman & Holman, 1996.

Blomberg, Craig. *The New American Commentary: Matthew.* Nashville, TN: Broadman & Holman Publishers, 1992.

Boa, Kenneth, and William Kruidenier. *Holman New Testament Commentary: Romans.* Nashville: Broadman & Holman, 2000.

Borchert, Gerald L. *The New American Commentary: John 1-11.* Nashville, TN: Broadman & Holman Publishers, 2001.

Borchert, Gerald L. *The New American Commentary vol. 25B, John 12-21.* Nashville: Broadman & Holman Publishers, 2002.

Brand, Chad, Charles Draper, and England Archie. *Holman Illustrated Bible Dictionary: Revised, Updated and Expanded.* Nashville, TN: Holman, 2003.

Breneman, Mervin. *The New American Commentary, vol. 10, Ezra, Nehemiah, Esther.* Nashville: Broadman & Holman Publishers, 1993.

Bromiley, Geoffrey W. *The International Standard Bible Encyclopedia (Vol. 1-4).* Grand Rapids, MI: William B. Eerdmans Publishing Co., 1986.

Bromiley, Geoffrey W., and Gerhard Friedrich. *Theological Dictionary of the New Testament, ed. Gerhard Kittel, vol. 4.* Grand Rapids, MI: Eerdmans, 1964-.

Brooks, James A. *The New American Commentary: Mark (Volume 23).* Nashville: Broadman & Holman Publishers, 1992.

Butler, Trent C. *Holman New Testament Commentary: Luke.* Nashville, TN: Broadman & Holman Publishers, 2000.

Butler, Trent C. *Holman Old Testament Commentary - Hosea, Joel, Amos, Obadiah, Jonah, Micah.* Nashville: Broadman & Holman Publishers, 2005.

Cole, R. Dennis. *THE NEW AMERICAN COMMENTARY: Volume 3b Numbers.* Nashville: Broadman & Holman Publishers, 2000.

Cooper, Lamar Eugene. *The New American Commentary, Ezekiel, vol. 17.* Nashville, TN: Broadman & Holman Publishers, 1994.

Cooper, Rodney. *Holman New Testament Commentary: Mark.* Nashville: Broadman & Holman Publishers, 2000.

Cornwall, Judson, and Stelman Smith. *The Exhaustive Dictionary of Bible Names.* Gainsville: Bridge-Logos, 1998.

Easley, Kendell H. *Holman New Testament Commentary, vol. 12, Revelation.* (Nashville, TN: Broadman & Holman Publishers, 1998.

Easton, M. G. *Easton's Bible Dictionary.* Oak Harbor, WA: Logos Research Systems, 1996, c1897.

Elwell, Walter A. *Baker Encyclopedia of the Bible.* Grand Rapids: Baker Book House, 1988.

—. *Evangelical Dictionary of Theology (Second Edition).* Grand Rapids: Baker Academic, 2001.

Elwell, Walter A, and Philip Wesley Comfort. *Tyndale Bible Dictionary.* Wheaton, Ill: Tyndale House Publishers, 2001.

Erickson, Millard J. *The Concise Dictionary of Christian Theology.* Wheaton: Crossway Books, 2001.

Fields, Lee M. *Hebrew For The Rest of Us: Using Hebrew Tools Without Mastering Biblical Hebrew.* Grand Rapids, MI: Zondervan, 2008.

Freedman, David Noel, Allen C. Myers, and Astrid B. Beck. *Eerdmans Dictionary of the Bible .* Grand Rapids, Mich.: W.B. Eerdmans , 2000.

Gangel, Kenneth O. *Holman New Testament Commentary: Acts.* Nashville, TN: Broadman & Holman Publishers, 1998.

Gangel, Kenneth O. *Holman New Testament Commentary, vol. 4, John .* Nashville, TN: Broadman & Holman Publishers, 2000.

—. *Holman Old Testament Commentary: Daniel.* Nashville: Broadman & Holman Publishers, 2001.

Garrett, Duane A. *Proverbs, Ecclesiastes, Song of Songs, The New American Commentary, vol. 14.* Nashville: Broadman & Holman Publishers, 1993.

—. *The New American Commentary: Vol. 14 (Proverbs, Ecclesiastes, Song of Songs).* Nashville: Broadman & Holman Publishers, 1993.

Geisler, Norman L. *Baker Encyclopedia of Christian Apologetics.* Grand Rapids: Baker Books, 1999.

George, Timothy. *The New American Commentary: Galatians .* Nashville, TN: Broadman & Holman Publishers, 2001.

Green, Joel B, Scot McKnight, and Howard Marshall. *Dictionary of Jesus and the Gospels.* Downers Grove, IL: InterVarsity Press, 1992.

Hastings, James, John A Selbie, and John C Lambert. *A Dictionary of Christ and the Gospels.* New York, NY: Charles Scribner's Sons, 1907.

Larson, Knute. *Holman New Testament Commentary, vol. 9, I & II Thessalonians, I & II Timothy, Titus, Philemon.* Nashville, TN: Broadman & Holman Publishers, 2000.

Lea, Thomas D. *Holman New Testament Commentary: Vol. 10, Hebrews, James.* Nashville, TN: Broadman & Holman Publishers, 1999.

Lea, Thomas D., and Hayne P. Griffin. *The New American Commentary, vol. 34, 1, 2 Timothy, Titus.* Nashville: Broadman & Holman Publishers, 1992.

Martin, D Michael. *The New American Commentary 33 1, 2 Thessalonians.* Nashville, TN: Broadman & Holman, 2001, c1995.

Martin, Glen S. *Holman Old Testament Commentary: Numbers.* Nashville: Broadman & Holman Publishers, 2002.

Mathews, K. A. *The New American Commentary vol. 1A, Genesis 1-11:26.* Nashville: Broadman & Holman Publishers, 2001.

Matthews, K. A. *The New American Commentary Vol. 1B, Genesis 11:27-50:26.* Nashville: Broadman and Holman Publishers, 2001.

Melick, Richard R. *The New American Commentary: vol. 32, Philippians, Colissians, Philemon.* Nashville, TN : Broadman & Holman Publishers, 2001.

Microsoft. *Encarta ® World English Dictionary.* Redmond: Microsoft Corporation, 1998-2010.

Miller, Stephen R. *The New American Commentary: Volume 18 Daniel.* Nashville: Broadman & Holman Publishers, 1994.

Mirriam-Webster, Inc. *Mirriam-Webster's Collegiate Dictionary. Eleventh Edition.* Springfield: Mirriam-Webster, Inc., 2003.

Mounce, Robert H. *Romans: The New American Commentary 27.* Nashville: Broadman & Holman, 2001, c1995.

Mounce, William D. *Mounce's Complete Expository Dictionary of Old & New Testament Words.* Grand Rapids, MI: Zondervan, 2006.

Myers, Allen C. *The Eerdmans Bible Dictionary .* Grand Rapids, Mich: Eerdmans, 1987.

Polhill, John B. *The New American Commentary 26: Acts.* Nashville: Broadman & Holman Publishers, 2001.

Pratt Jr, Richard L. *Holman New Testament Commentary: I & II Corinthians, vol. 7.* Nashville: Broadman & Holman Publishers, 2000.

Richardson, Kurt. *The New American Commentary Vol. 36 James.* Nashville: Broadman & Holman Publishers, 1997.

Rooker, Mark F. *The New American Commentary, vol. 3A, Leviticus.* Nashville: Broadman & Holman Publishers, 2000.

—. *Holman Old Testament Commentary: Ezekiel.* Nashville: Broadman & Holman Publishers, 2005.

Schreiner, Thomas R. *The New American Commentary: 1, 2 Peter, Jude.* Nashville: Broadman & Holman, 2003.

Smith, Gary. *The New American Commentary: Isaiah 1-39, Vol. 15a.* Nashville, TN: B & H Publishing Group, 2007.

—. *The New American Commentary: Isaiah 40-66, Vol. 15b.* Nashville, TN: B&H Publishing, 2009.

Stein, Robert H. *The New American Commentary: Luke.* Nashville, TN: Broadman & Holman , 2001, c1992.

Stuart, Douglas K. *The New American Commentary: An Exegetical Theological Exposition of Holy Scripture EXODUS.* Nashville: Broadman & Holman, 2006.

Taylor, Richard A, and Ray E Clendenen. *The New American Commentary: Haggai, Malachi, , vol. 21A .* Nashville, TN: Broadman & Holman Publishers, 2007.

Vine, W E. *Vine's Expository Dictionary of Old and New Testament Words.* Nashville: Thomas Nelson, 1996.

Walls, David, and Max Anders. *Holman New Testament Commentary: I & II Peter, I, II & III John, Jude.* Nashville: Broadman & Holman Publishers, 1996.

Weber, Stuart K. *Holman New Testament Commentary, vol. 1, Matthew.* Nashville, TN: Broadman & Holman Publishers, 2000.

Wood, D R W. *New Bible Dictionary (Third Edition).* Downers Grove: InterVarsity Press, 1996.

Zodhiates, Spiros. *The Complete Word Study Dictionary: New Testament.* Chattanooga: AMG Publishers, 2000, c1992, c1993.

www.ingramcontent.com/pod-product-compliance
Lightning Source LLC
Chambersburg PA
CBHW022107040426
42451CB00007B/156